THE AVERAGE MAN

SUMIIT TRIPATHY

CONTENTS

AVERAGE

Hi, I am the Average Man. I am guessing that if you are reading this, you are also average, just like me. Born in an average family, not too rich, not too poor. Average at studies and average at sports, but the only thing we both have that makes us relate to each other is that we have a dream. That is the only thing in our life that is not average. We both have a dream to do something big in life, to get out of the average life and live big and extraordinary lives. Now, I am not planning for this book to be a bestseller of some sort, but all I am planning to do while writing this book is figure out how to get out of being **average**. Now, both you and I aren't exceptionally talented at anything, but we know our end goal is waiting for us. Just don't know how to get there. Now I am quite selfish and am going to write this book to figure out my life and get my shit together. But I am hoping as I figure my shit out, I also end up forming a guide to getting out of this average cycle. A guide to being extraordinary. If you have picked up this book and are ready for some self-experimentation, then let's do it together.

But before we both are truly ready to get out of an ordinary life, let me tell you why I want to do this. Sure, you will have your own reasons, or maybe our reasons are the same; I honestly don't know. I don't want this life anymore cause I am missing out on so many new and different life experiences. If it is true and we just actually have one life, I got to kill the average man inside me who loves the comfort zone, is never ready to change life for the better, and feels like nothing will ever change. I am truly convinced that if I continue my life the way it is right now, I will not be able to live much longer. I feel suffocated and locked in this cage, where I know I have the resources to build a key and get out, but self-doubt just isn't letting me get there. I know that even if I make it out of this lifestyle, I won't feel happier than I normally do or more fulfilled because those things are intrinsic, and you need to work on those aspects of your life separately, but the stuff I can experience and the freedom I will get will be tenfold.

Now, I have always wanted to do something creative, just don't know what. I gave up on finding a purpose a long time ago. You can't just have one purpose in life, can you? I think the purpose of life is to live each moment, and nothing else really matters. I have found that living life like a bucket list of things I want to do is working out for me. Sure, my bucket list is always going to be infinite, and so is yours, but living the day is what matters. I have had those days where I wished I was a little bit more confident to talk to a certain person, make a new friend, or just randomly compliment someone. Now, those are small but not so ordinary things as our generation doesn't even have the balls to talk to the person in front of us.

As an average man, I have also never felt the feeling of truly accomplishing something significant. I also feel like a loser sometimes and question why things aren't going my way. The thought of loneliness also haunts me just like it does to everyone else. Well, honestly, that's ok cause we all feel these things, regardless of if we are rich or poor. The thing that I have noticed about us "Common men" is that we are filled with a lot of envy. We are less grateful for the stuff we have and only focus on the stuff we don't have, making us feel eternally average. Maybe there is no one definition of success or no one path towards it. But generally, If you are having a better life and are able to get most of the things you want in life, you are pretty successful. Why is it that so few people in the world have actually reached there? Aren't they just people like us? What makes them have a much superior lifestyle If they have the brains, Intellect and Human Body just like us? The obvious answer is that they took more risks in life than us, but that can't be all now, can it? Feels like a lot of elements from their success stories are missing. Maybe it was the environment, maybe it was the ego or just purely talent.

People really despise the word **EGO.** They think it's a negative quality in people. I used to believe this for a long time before I actually took a step back and noticed that every successful person has a little bit of ego mixed in their personality. If you know how to harness your ego, you can unlock new skills. Personally, since I am average, I don't consider my ego a part of my personality yet. As the first part of my self-experimentation, I am going to intentionally practice a bit of ego in my personality. Ego should help me push myself to my limits and potentially get good at every activity I pick up. You have to read the next chapter to know if this actually worked. Cause if this actually does work, then maybe you can implement it in your life, too. In order to measure my progress more accurately. I will strictly use ego for things I am not actually good at. For now, I will measure my 3 criteria which I wanted to always be good at but suck, to be honest. You can choose 3 things in your life and follow along.

The 3 things I will be choosing for this ego experiment are Chess, Guitar and Graphic design. Here is what I am going to do. Since focusing on all 3 things at once is going to be futile as the ego can only handle one thing at a time. For the first 3 months, I am going to focus on chess while practising the other 2 things in a non-intense way. I call this active ego practice and passive ego practice. The main difference is that I am actively going to try getting better at chess, watching videos on the subject, studying about it and obsessing about it. I am going to subconsciously assume I am the best and play each game of chess as if it were my final match. A combination of obsession and ego should theoretically give me the desired motivation to be better at it. As a wise man once said, "Obsession is a blend of Ego and Passion".

Here is my current skill chart in the 3 things I am going to do

Chess	Guitar	Graphic Design
Rating 760-800	Just know a few open Chords	Just Downloaded Photoshop with no clue how to use it

Here is your current skill chart (fill it out and follow along)

THE EGO

The Ego is a wonderful thing if you play your cards right. It's been 3 months since I wrote the last chapter and before I tell you more I am ecstatic about my progress. Here is what my progress chart looks like right now.

Chess	Guitar	Graphic Design
Got my Rating Up To the 980 Range	I learned a few Bar Chords but the next 3 months are for music practice	Still struggling but can make basic designs in Photoshop

Now to give you some context on how much better I have got at chess, because I assume all of you don't play. 980 Rating is the highest I have ever been. Although my goal is to be 1000+, with the help of my ego and constant practice, I pushed myself beyond what I could have achieved earlier. My ego enabled me to start playing with computer bots and slowly learning new techniques to beat them. My ego helped me find other chess players who were better than me and try to beat them. In the start, I lost almost every game I played. Most people without an ego would give up and try something new, but somehow, my ego gave me this feeling of frustration that made me play more and more games. Ego has always been perceived as a negative expression of self, but once we flip it and make it a means of motivation, progress is evident.

How has Your Progress been?

Be careful, though, because ego has always been a double-edged sword. If you make progress, never think that you are the best and stop with your efforts. The solution to that is to look in the mirror and try telling yourself that you got to be better than you were yesterday. A sanguine hope is created once you start taking the skills you want to develop as a game of progress. To get better at something, humans need time, in fact, a lot of time. We can't learn as fast as AI or skip the progress and jump to our goals. But all that fighting keeps our destination fresh, and once we reach it, we have a new goal to triumph.

Now that my 3 months with chess are over, I am going to move to guitar and singing for my next 3 months. Even though my guitar skills have progressed, I am an absolute beginner at singing. I am sure you are also ready to move on to your next skill. Now, when I say move on to your next skill, I don't mean that you completely leave the skill you worked so hard on for the last 3 months. Do that on autopilot, like during your leisure time or whenever the mood feels like it. Treat it as a passive thing. If you like, you can also continue with the same skill for the next 3 months, but that might become too monotonous. Variety keeps us motivated in life. That's why I follow this strategy.

Harnessing the Ego the Right Way

It is easy to get carried away and stray from your goal when there is an ego involved. There are two streams of thought when it comes to the ego. One is that "I am the best, and that is why I don't need to put much work into this" or "I am the best, but other people are out to get me and are also improving, so I got to work my hardest". Finding a worthy competitor helps. Someone who is good but not so good that you can't surpass him or her with time, practice and dedication. Once you beat that person, you gain more confidence, and your ego is also boosted. Then you can find somebody else whose skills you would like to match. The best part is you don't even have to tell them that they are your competition. You can just play this game in your mind. Some people have talent, and there is no doubt about it, but talent is no substitute for hard work. In fact, things can work out great even with 0 talent but a hell of a lot of hard work.

Most people think that the learning curve or progress curve is always uniform, but this is simply not true. There will be moments where your progress goes down, or you get stuck at some point. If these moments aren't there, you simply have not learned enough to get there.

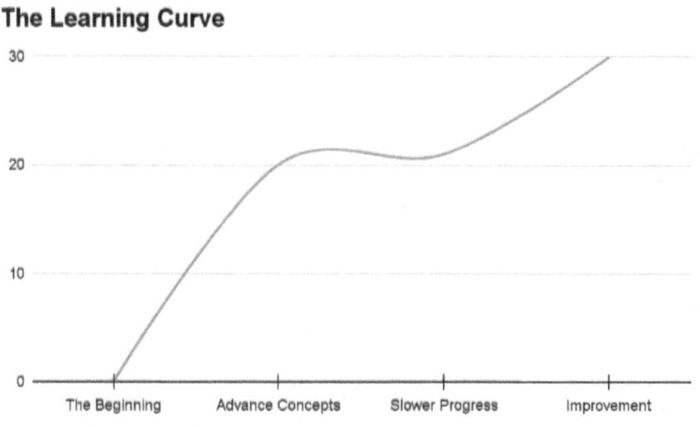

To get ahead in the curve, you have to give it time and be consistent. The combination of the two is, however, not enough. Learning has to be structured with newer concepts being introduced with time to improve in any skill. It will be tempting to quit after a certain level, but progress takes conscious effort.

So initially, as a beginner, when you start learning a new skill, it comes off as easier than it actually is. This is because you are grasping the basics first. Now, this will boost your confidence heavily, but as you progress, let's say a month or two, your learning rate will decrease as the deeper you go into the subject, the more complex it will feel, like wading through a storm. The good news is if you make it through this stage, you will attain a decent grip on the skill you are trying to learn. This will make you above average, as most people give up at this stage, and that's where the learning curve is.

FAME

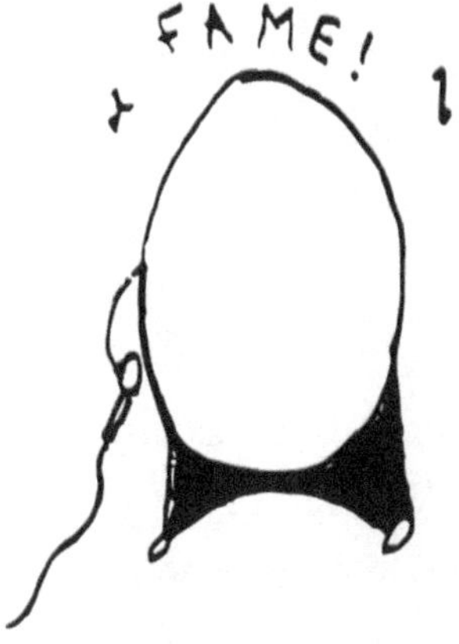

A few years ago, everything I used to do was in the hopes of getting the sweet taste of **fame**. That got me nowhere. Sure, you could say my consistency improved, but my joy of learning just went away. I created content, and it went from "I want to really talk about this today with my audience" to "Why didn't I get views on this video?". Fame just creates totally unnecessary pressure on you that stops you from doing the stuff that actually matters to you. I call this pseudo fame, as making the stuff people will like is never as good as people appreciating your work cause it's different. It's ironic how the ego can be a superpower while fame can destroy everything you have. Now, is fame bad? No, not at all; fame is basically being so good at the stuff you do that unknown people are inspired by it. Never use this as a tool of measurement, though, because once you start to do that, your confidence in your ability plummets faster than the price of the dogecoin. Think about it this way: if you think your end goal is to get good at something without seeking validation from others, you will eventually get validation as a plus point.

It's just like the Buddhist concept of sometimes doing nothing to get something. Here you don't actively pursue fame but it comes to you as a by-product of getting good at the stuff you learn. Find joy in learning instead of ever worrying if you will ever be good enough. Trust me it gets a lot of weight out of your chest.

Well, most people reading this book won't be convinced that **Fame = Unnecessary Pressure** because the average man is tired of always being average and wants to stand out. That is understandable and alright. The drive for fame can be a positive thing if it's just a want and doesn't become a need. Fame is the trickiest thing. It first makes you believe that you want it more than anything else in the world, and when you get it, all sorts of people slam their opinions about you.

Ed Sheeran once said, and I quote, "Success doesn't teach you shit, it never has, but a 100 failures will teach you way more." Now, life is never going to be a smooth sailing ship; it has never been and never will be, but the pain and struggle make it all feel meaningful in the end. Not to go all Bollywood on you, but "Kaamyaab hone ke liye nahin, Kaabil hone ke liye padho!" this translates to "Don't learn to be successful but rather learn to master the skill."

Fame is fun for a while but soon it gets annoying. It gives you a sense of false power and chances are that if you are reading this book. You want to be anything but average in life. Chasing superficial fame will surely not get you there.

Only the bold minds are ever remembered. When Freddie Mercury walked into the radio stations with his song Bohemian Rhapsody, NOBODY was ready to play it. They said it was way too long to be a song on the radio. Ironically, it was one of "Queen's Greatest Hits". Well, don't confuse bold with stupid, though, or it could land you in big trouble. The average man wants to wear the shimmering tag of success but isn't willing to pay the price for it. Anyone can go from average to great with enough time and consistency.

Recognition comes afterwards. Think of it this way: you aren't famous now only because you are preparing and getting ready to handle it. You are getting ready for greatness. You are a diamond in the rough. With each day you work towards learning, you polish your diamond and make it shine. If you do something long enough, you will be good at it without even really trying.

I want you to look at the newspaper boy or maybe street food vendors. They have been doing the same craft for years and years to a point where even normal things like cutting vegetables are done with so much grace and finesse. Most of them remain unknown masters. Learning without any expectations is the best kind of learning you can do. Set reasonable goals; in fact, the smaller the goal, the better. With each goal you achieve, never forget to celebrate your milestone. Remember, all you have to do is be better than you were yesterday, and you will never ever remain average.

Life will always give you opportunities. You just have to grab them when you are ready. When you create, people will start to take notice. This may require years and years of hopeless practice sessions, but when you strike gold, the gold shall keep coming. It will come all at once, and people will call you an overnight success story, but only you will know the sleepless nights you spent on this overnight success story.

MENTAL CONDITIONING

All our lives we have been trained to follow rules. Do you remember the sense of freedom and encouragement you had as a kid? Well you are an adult now and when you spent all your life fitting in now you are just to scared to stand out anymore. This is the mental conditioning society has done to us. You ever wonder, why it's so hard to get out of the comfortzone? It's not because you don't want to but rather you are told not to.

Told by who? Literally, everyone who "cares about you". Your parents, your teachers, and even your friends.

This is because getting out of your comfort zone is not something they did. So they let their past experiences dictate your life. The way out of average needs you to take many risks in life. To go all in and truly believe in yourself. But from a young age, we are taught not to take risks because you might get screwed over and fall flat on your face. Let me tell you one thing that might change your perspective on this. "Death is the only certainty in life." Nothing else in between is certain. Playing it safe may also have uncertainties, just like taking risks. So, if everything is uncertain, then why not take that first step and explore? I live by a very strong motto. My motto is, "You have to fuck around to find out."

Getting out of your comfort zone requires you to be a yes man. Whenever someone has pitched me an idea they are deeply passionate about, I have said yes to them almost every time, sometimes even when I don't completely agree with them. Each time I say yes, I take myself out of the comfort zone and explore a new idea, and learn something regardless of failure or success.

The trick to getting out of your comfort zone is to be naive. A hopeful optimist can achieve way more than a negative Nancy because they just simply try more things. In these past years, saying yes has helped me learn skills like negotiation, understanding people, clothing design, and many more. If you want to truly know your full potential, then you have to let go of your current beliefs. If we listen to everyone's advice every time we try something new, we will never be able to try new things.

The main reason people don't get out of their comfort zone is fear. But let me tell you that your fear is irrational and usually is based on somebody else's experience rather than your own. When you try to actually understand the core reason behind your fear, you will observe that it is blown out of proportion in your head. When I started my public speaking coaching, my fear was that I wasn't good enough, and that fear stayed with me, so I did something I call productive procrastination. It may sound like a positive thing, but it's not. This is basically when you do unnecessary tasks to keep yourself busy, but they don't help you reach your goal in any way. I remember sitting for hours on the computer and trying to make the best poster for my classes. This may seem productive at first, but when you really look at it from the client's point of view, They only care about how you can help them reach their goal, not which font you used in your poster.

Our brain is very good at deception and will do anything to keep us in our comfort zone because of factors like our upbringing and inbuilt survival mechanisms. This means the only way to beat our minds at deception is to play our own tricks on it.

How Do I Do That?

To trick thousands of years of evolution is surprisingly simple. Instead of focusing on outcomes, focus on the processes. If your goal is to make a million dollars, focus on writing down the ideas that will help you get there, and focus on building the skills to get there. Do the boring stuff instead of chasing the fancy stuff since every big goal requires hours of doing boring stuff to get there. Here is the thing about willpower: it strengthens with each uncomfortable task you do. This isn't motivational bullshit but rather science. There is a part of the brain called the Anterior mid-cingulate cortex that controls your willpower and attention span. Believe it or not, it gets stronger when you do uncomfortable and "hard" tasks. When this part of your brain is trained, you can become a high-performing individual, in other words, above average. So the next time you don't feel like doing something, think of it as strengthening your brain and do the task. The more you do, the stronger your will to do more becomes.

DON'T BE A MACHINE

What has 2 legs, 2 arms and a mind? It's "YOU" stupid. We may all be born with the same organs, but it's our minds that make us different. Use it right, and average would never be an option. Use it wrong and you are stuck in the loop forever. Most people treat themselves like machines. 80-hour work weeks, barely any sleep, food that can barely even be classified as food and of course, the endless scrolling through social media, wondering why their life isn't going anywhere. How will you ever get the time to learn the stuff that actually matters to you? How will you ever be who you really want to be? Now, I can give you general advice by saying: cut down on scrolling, use the weekends to work on yourself, etc., but guess what? That doesn't work for most people, including me. I just can't live without watching reels on Instagram or enjoying the weekends. So what's the solution? Don't be a Machine. Yes, you can't expect to cut down everything you love and cherish, but you can sabotage your brain by thinking it's relaxing while you are actually learning.

Smart right? So, instead of mindlessly scrolling through Instagram, how about you follow some pages that teach or at least talk about the skills you want to improve? Even if you mindlessly scroll through these pieces of content, you are still learning subconsciously. Now, obviously, you won't remember everything you learn while you are in relax mode, but you can always go back to those videos while actively learning.

Living for the weekend is the most bullshit idea. You know why? Because I prefer living my life the way I want, every single fucking day. So I say live every day, and also, while you enjoy life, add some learning or practice every day so that you can enjoy your days in a balanced way. You may not be as dedicated as Koby Bryant or Elon Musk but just be dedicated enough to show up for practice at least 80% of the time. It's a low bar but better than giving up completely. Let's make this even easier. In the 80% of the time that you show up, you don't even have to practice for hours. Just 5 minutes. You can go beyond that if you want, but just 5 minutes of practice 80% of the time would help you learn and take your skills to the next level without much effort. When the bar is that low, it almost hurts your ego when you don't do it. You start feeling worthless for not even being able to achieve the bare minimum, and this fear keeps you going in life. It keeps compounding your skills over time.

Some days are going to be gloomy when you try learning something. The days where you question yourself, saying, "Is this even worth it?" Let me tell you that those days matter the most. Anyone can work hard on the days when they are teeming with creative energy and motivation, but working on those days where you feel like, "Is this even worth it?" you have to remind yourself that it is.

Work on the Current you for the Future you.

Our small actions affect us in a large way over time. This is what's called compounding. When we do something for someone else, we somehow are twice as motivated to do so. But when it comes to doing stuff for us, we barely even care. Spend time in Solitude, and Thou shall reap the reward.

Only when we let ourselves free to explore and learn, disconnect from society for a while to be alone with our thoughts, can we achieve progress.

You need to give up the destination and simply focus on the journey. Don't focus on what will happen, but start to savour the journey. The ordinary everyday practices make an extraordinary talent. Learning something new is like a jigsaw puzzle. You have to find the pieces and put them in the right places to finally see the whole picture. When we start the puzzle, it's mostly just trial and error, not really knowing what we intend to do, but as the pieces mix and match, picturesque scenery is unravelled.

Machines may be able to learn new skills in seconds, but you, as an average man, have to trust the process. If the process is right, then you will eventually get to the finish line, but if you mess up the process, you will never really move to the next level or go above average. I will talk more about this in the next chapter.

FORCED LEARNING

Learning should be fun. We all have heard this, and it's an idea I also believe in, but then what's forced learning? You can't force yourself to have fun, right? I believe learning can never be perfunctory, but you can force yourself to learn something while having fun with it. How do you do that? That is what we all want to know the answer to, so I shall not gatekeep. It's quite simple, actually: you can force yourself to learn something by putting something you already love into the picture. Huh? What does that mean? Don't worry. By the end of this chapter, I can guarantee you that learning a new skill will be easier than ever.

So, let's say you want to learn to sing. Now, you can try on your own, but you will eventually run out of motivation to continue. This is where forced learning comes into play. If you want to learn to sing, you have to think like a musician and simply copy their routine and behaviour. I would approach learning a new skill in a way that can give me rewards while I learn it. The rewards I get have to be directly proportional to the amount I learn. This way, I can simply force myself to get better and earn better rewards. The only thing is the rewards have to be regular and actually something you desire and look forward to. Let's come back to singing. The first thing I did was hire an instructor that I liked so that he could hold me accountable for the progress I make and also help me with my consistency. Now, here is where things get tricky. You can find a lot of instructors out there, but the trick is to choose the best one for you instead of the cheapest one. Now, every field has instructors who can teach you whatever you desire to learn using a structured approach. The good thing about not hiring a cheap instructor is the quality of their teaching, as well as the guilt attached to missing their sessions, as you will lose money. This way, you have to force yourself to be consistent or risk losing out on the money you pay to hire an instructor.

If you are broke and can't really afford an instructor, try to associate yourself with a mentor. Mentors are a little hard to find, but it's best to find people who are slightly better than you and can teach you enough to get started. Your goal should be to get better than your mentors. So find people who are just one or two levels better than you and are learning as well. This method of forced learning also taps into your ego, which drives you crazy, giving you the motivation to be better than them. These people can be your friends, coworkers, or hell, they don't even have to know that you are competing with them. Once you become better than your mentor, it's time to find a new one. Competition helps you learn skills a lot faster than if you were to do it alone.

Now, there's another approach to forced learning, which is the complete opposite of this. In this situation, you try to teach the skill you are learning to others. Obviously, you wouldn't yet be good enough to charge for it, but you can start creating content around it. Weirdly enough, the more you teach, the more you learn. As you continue to go from teaching basic concepts while simultaneously learning more advanced concepts over the months, you can monetise them in the form of courses or special services. The best part of this approach is you force yourself to learn just so that you can teach others. One thing I have noticed is that when we try to do stuff that involves other people, we tend not to screw it up in order to save our reputation in the public eye. Although we should learn to extricate ourselves from judgement, sometimes judgement forces us to learn and improve ourselves.

Both these approaches can work out really well for you. However, I personally recommend trying a mix of both. Teaching will help you remember what you learned, and a teacher will help you reach your full potential. I have tried forced learning for years now. It has never disappointed me. That's because humans love talking about stuff they know in order to fit into society and show off. It's a win-win situation; you get to learn and inspire people who are new to the field to learn along with you. Nobody goes from zero to hero in a day or two; it takes consistency, and sadly, motivation isn't always enough to get you to where you want to be, so figuring out tips and tricks to just show up for practice is the best way to get better at things you want to learn in life.

Now I want you to make a list of things you want to force learn. Fill them in the table below and by the end of this book I want you to use the steps I teach in this book to become consistent at the things you do. Just show up most days.

Things you want to Learn	Forced learning approach you used

The goal should always be clear and attractive enough for forced learning to work. You can always trick your brain to work with effort and consistency instead of a more perfunctory and half hearted approach to learning. Personally, nowadays whenever I try learning a new skill I use Chat GPT to give me a step by step plan on getting to my goals. This makes my approach much more streamlined and easy to work on.

There is a secret sauce to forced learning that can make the process much easier for you. It's so simple but takes a little conscious effort.

THE RIGHT CROWD

Did you know that you gain the qualities of the top 5 people you talk to on a regular basis? Well, this is the most generic advice: "Surround yourself with the right people". But who are the right people, and how do we find them? You might think, well, I can just connect with them on Instagram or find people with common interests at work. Well, that doesn't work as well as it sounds in theory. Usually, you talk once or twice about the things you are interested in, or maybe there is a big knowledge gap, which can be super overwhelming, or if you are on the other side of the conversation, it is super boring. Why should people give you their time? Would you do that if a stranger DM's you?

All of it is okay in the background, but to truly find the kind of people who are at your level, you have to be unconventional. Want to learn cooking? Offer to help at a soup kitchen or walk around good local street food stalls and try the food as well as strike up a conversation with them. The truth is you don't have to actively learn the skill 24\7. Observing the masters of the craft is also subconscious learning. Want to learn to sing? Go to the church, start singing along with the crowd, and talk to the choir. Want to learn public speaking? Join debates or try getting on stage more often. Want to learn investing? Just walk into a finance summit. Unconventional ways indeed, but the best ways to form real connections.

Conversation leads to connections. Most importantly, when you go to places where people of all experiences and walks of life unite, you find your tribe. Some connections are better than others, but they take time to develop. It will definitely feel weird at first to try out these things, but once you realise that nobody really knows you at these places and if things go wrong, you can always escape the situation without facing any consequences, you are truly free here to be you without caring about the people who judge. People will always judge, but it definitely helps if you don't ever have to meet those people again. The best part is that with the practice you get from forced learning, you will eventually feel like you fit in these places and will have some very interesting conversations and learning experiences.

The right crowd is different for everyone. Now, if you are a total beginner at something and you go hang out with the pros, then both you and they will get bored, and no real connection will be formed. Instead, if you decide to approach people who are just slightly better than you, then both you and the other person can have relatable conversations. However, keep in mind that you should try talking to at least one professional in the skill you are trying to learn to get motivated and see what you yourself could blossom to one day.

I know this is totally off topic but yesterday I finally made it to a 1000 rating in chess, Just wanted to share the good news with all of you. So my 3 month chess goal is complete. Now I can choose to replace it with something else or set a new chess goal. I have chosen to replace it with something else I have been trying to learn for a long time but never get the time. That is face drawings and getting over all better at drawing.

New Goal: Learn to draw male and female faces that look aesthetic and anatomically accurate.

How are your goals going? Did you complete any of them yet? You can share your progress in the box below and also remember it is important to look back every once in a while or else it just feels like an endless repetition with no real progress.

Your Progress with your Goals

Anyway, back to connections. These connections help you improve but in the long run they can also land you gigs and opportunities once you get good enough at what you are trying to learn. Imagine how cool it is to learn something as well as make money from it just by finding the right mentors and company to hang out with.

Now, half of my readers must be thinking... but what if I am an introvert? I hate talking to new people.

Well, you are right. Most people who actually try to master something or get really good at something are introverts, as they simply practice out of boredom. At least that is the case with me; yes, you heard that right: I am an introvert as well, and I hate talking to new people as much as you do. But the best part about talking to new people is that their opinion isn't worth a dime to you. You can just leave if you don't vibe with the people you talk to. Also, nobody said your tribe has to be physically present. It's 2023. A simple Reddit search would take you to thousands of people with the same goal and skill level as you. Sure, some would be better or worse, but who cares? It would still be you sharing your work and opinion without having to ever see those people in real life.

So now you literally have no excuses not to connect with new people. I also used to make these excuses prior to my learning journey. When I realised that the only person I was fooling was myself. I stopped caring about what other people thought or if I would ever be famous. All that mattered was to be so good at something that the people around me could not help but notice. Mindset changes motivation. When you literally put yourselves in high-stake situations where you have to do or die, you will be forced to push yourselves to the limits you thought you could never reach before. Progress or Perish is my new life mantra that keeps me driven. It means if I stop with my progress, it will slowly decay and perish with the passage of time. Since I don't want my past efforts to go to waste, I need to continue to make progress.

Talent is just being at the right place at the right time. I want you to remember a memory of how you fell in love with your favourite sport or maybe your favourite hobby. Everyone has those core memories, even though they can be a little blurry. Now imagine that day if you weren't at that exact spot with the right people who encouraged you through your first goal or first artwork or the first time you played an instrument. Even if you were probably terrible at it, the people around you made it seem like you were the best in the world, and that memory will keep you driven for life. It will show you a future where you might as well be the best in the world. Your work means nothing if you don't show it to the right people.

Let me take my own example because why not? Whenever I sang to my friends, they said it was horrible no matter how much I practised. On the contrary, when I sang the same thing to my vocal instructor, he told me that it needed work but wasn't as bad as I thought. He pointed out the exact things I did right, and to be honest, nothing felt more motivating than that single moment. I am not quite there yet, but at least I know I won't be stopping any time soon. The right people actually know what they are talking about and know how you can be better at whatever you are trying to learn because, let's face it, they have also passed the exact same stages as you. So they can relate to you. The untrained crowd just cares about the result and not the process to get there.

FROM AVERAGE TO ABOVE AVERAGE

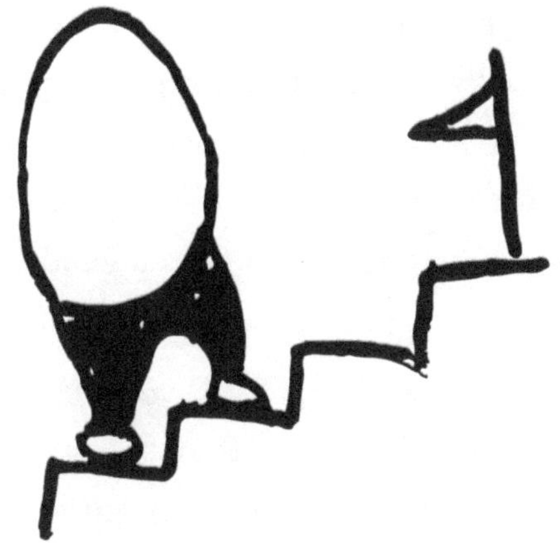

Before we start, I have to tell you something important. When you feel average, there is always going to be someone who thinks you are above average. No matter how much you suck at something, I want you to truly believe this. Since you have no way of proving my statement wrong, you might as well believe it. No matter how good you are, trust me, after a point of time, you will start feeling average, and that is the beauty of it. There is always new insight to gain on the skill you want to learn.

Everyone keeps waiting to be the best, but they forget to look at the progress they have made. Learning is a journey without a destination. Well, now that, that is out of the way, let's make you go from "I suck at this" to "I am better than most people will ever be".

Practice, practice, practice is what they all say but I think what they mean is consistent, consistent and consistent. Just by simply showing up everyday you are already ahead of 90% of the people trying to get better at something. The other 10% which is the secret sauce will be explicated by me and you in this chapter.

But first, let's talk about this beautiful thing called compounding. In math class, if you remember, you studied compound interest, and all I remember is that it was the most boring thing on this entire planet. Just a few years ago, though, I began to see compounding in real life, and it was beautiful. Compounding, in simple terms, is when your earnings get extra interest due to the previous year's earnings, which are also added to calculate the new interest earned. Didn't understand? Well, it basically means that whatever shit you do in life adds up in one way or the other for better or for worse. When you learn stuff for a year, the tasks you took a lot of time to properly do take away less of your time now. This is because you have learned to do the task efficiently without any unnecessary steps being involved. So basically, your learning always keeps compounding, and the longer you do something, the faster you can do it.

People talk about motivation, about willpower but honestly just showing up most of the days will automatically get you where you want to be just because of compounding. It doesn't matter if you aren't fully focused because you can start over from scratch again tomorrow or revisit the work you are doing, in the future when you know better.

To get better, you will need to get worse. What the hell does that mean? Well, what I mean by this is that practice doesn't have to be pretty. You will fall a bit, and stuff will not come out perfectly. Learning is a graph filled with highs and lows. You may be at a stage where you have the potential to achieve your goal, but you aren't brave enough to jeopardise your success. I know it sounds counterproductive to do something even though it isn't your best work, but to take what you have learned and truly embed it in your subconscious, you need to focus on building muscle memory rather than perfectionism. Perfectionism is a great thing, and it is good advice to always try your best, but we can only do so much while we are conscious. True mastery is earned when you can perform those same tasks subconsciously or without putting much thought into it.

Show your best self to others and keep your worst to yourself. Now, by this, I mean that when you are showing someone your skill or your work, people do not care how you get there. They only and solely care about the result. I know people keep talking about sharing your process, and yada yada, but that is only when you are already an expert in your field. If you share your progress, no matter how much you have improved, sadly, no one gives a damn. So, don't share your practice, but rather share once you are really, really good enough because people are stupid and ludicrous. So, they will give their judgement and critique and bombard you with their unsolicited advice. People don't understand what work in progress is. Their words would thwart your success. So keep it to yourself and only ask those people who know something about the stuff you are learning, for advice.

The average mind always resists being above average cause we are stuck in our comfort zone. Is learning comfortable? I am going to be honest with you: **NO!** And that's not your fault. It is just how our brains have always evolved to prefer short-term success over long-term success; that is because cavemen didn't really have a future plan. I want you to take a moment to think about why it is that every time you start a diet or exercise, your body always feels like skipping. That is because you are literally going against thousands of years of evolution to rewire your brain. Any negative reinforcement can deeply affect you. Now, negativity will always be there, but if we look at it as an opportunity to prove someone wrong, it is a **Win** for us.

Be obsessed with the things you do, regardless of how good you are at them. It is much more satisfying to go from bad to good than to be just stuck at good and be cocky about it. The learning curve is needed to truly appreciate what you learn. Even Though everybody can not be obsessed with something, as we have a thousand worries to worry about, we can at least try to imagine what it would be like if we were the best at the thing that is currently being learned us.

Whenever I am practising drawing or singing or whatever, I just think of people looking at my fictional art gallery or listening to the best song ever, of course, made by me. If you can't actively obsess, you should at least try to fantasise about the endless doors that could open for you.

RESTART WHAT YOU FINISHED

We all have heard the famous saying, "Finish what you started," but while learning, there is no finish line you can reach and bask in your glory. Learning is Infinite because people just keep finding new things and new ways to do the same thing. It takes people a lifetime to attain mastery in a single field, but we are trying to get better at all the things we are interested in.

The trick is to put your full focus on that task for 3 months, then subconsciously practice it with lesser focus when you pick up your next skill to improve on. That way, you don't lose touch and actually push yourself forward. You need to press the resume button on those skills eventually, but the only difference is that each time you decide to resume a skill, your baseline is different and higher than from where you began. This way, it doesn't become monotonous, and you actually improve and progress. The key thing to remember while restarting a skill is to never do it alone. Join a discord community or a forum, or start with a friend. That way, you have somebody accountable for your actions because finding the motivation to restart a skill can be challenging.

A good strategy I use is performing the skill whether it is to make some extra cash or a stage performance. The truth is pressure motivates while being idle and free can make you lethargic.

I know we are talking about restarting a skill right now, but I really wanted to share that I have started to learn boxing from scratch. The reason for this was that I recently got assaulted and just couldn't feel safe after that. So, sometimes, even trauma can motivate us to learn and master new things. Our lows let us reach our highs because if there are no lows, we can never truly appreciate the highs.

Think of restarting a skill as an opportunity to level up and upgrade your horizon. It will let you look at what you learn from a different lens. We, as humans, are egoists, and we love to be fucking great at most things we do. To be great, you have to keep revisiting what you started. I have always thought of life as a simulation of consciousness. We are the heroes of our own story, and each of us sees reality differently. Our mind is the only barrier between us and our goals. Whenever you feel like giving up, I want you to consciously think about one thing that one of my mentors taught me, and I quote her: " Think of every problem you face in life as an opportunity and not a challenge". Honestly, this can save you a lot of unnecessary panic when life throws a problem at you. When you think of these quirks of life as opportunities, you are calm and automatically arrive at the solution quicker. The problem, or in our case the learning curve, is always exaggerated in our heads. I have found the solution staring at me right under my nose many times, but panic used to cloud my judgement. So nowadays, I just keep repeating in my head, "THINK OF IT AS AN OPPORTUNITY!!!" My panic automatically goes away, and life is much better without ludicrous rationalisation done by our panicking brains.

You should know when to press the restart button, tho. The golden rule is only to press the restart button on those skills that mean the most to you. We all have 24 hours, and if you subtract all the mundane tasks of life, it's really more like 5 to 8 hours. You need to accept that you will have to leave some skills behind, knowing in your heart that you're still better at it than most people ever could be. I would say when you are ready to restart skills, pick 3 skills max. Give your heart and soul to these 3 skills. You can use focused learning but also revisit those 3 skills specifically once a learning cycle is complete. For these 3 skills, our goal is to be so good that we could probably teach others that skill. Deep understanding is important, but you can't expect yourself to learn each and every skill deeply. The fact remains that you can easily go from 0 to above average at any skill if you follow the advice in this book. Trust me, average people always put in minimum effort. They almost never have a goal set for themselves and have a more go-with-the-flow attitude. You will never find an average man saying, "I want to be the best in the world" or "I hate losing to this guy". Basically, with time, we can become rusty if we learn too many skills. Don't get me wrong. If your training cycles are strong, the rusty you will also be good enough in the eyes of most people. However, it won't be the best version of you in that scenario. It mostly leaves you with an incomplete feeling, knowing that you can't do as much as you used to before. Spoiler alert " THAT FEELING SUCKS".

So even if you learn 10 skills, you need to keep revisiting them at least twice a year. This is so that our stupid brain doesn't put those skill sets in our short-term memory along with things like what you had for lunch last week or what you learned in 10th-grade chem class.

We usually tend to forget the skills we learned in around a time span of 5 years. By forgetting, I mean really stooping as low as a beginner. I will tell you the importance of revisiting skills with an example of my friend. So a friend of mine spent straight 5 years learning music (2 years of guitar and 3 years of keyboard). This is usually more than enough to be good at music, but then he left it for 5 years straight, and now if you ask him to play a keyboard, he just simply cannot, even though the same guy used to perform concerts as a kid. Well, good for you; revisiting skills every now and then will print them in your long-term memory, and eventually, it will become as natural to you as driving a car or brushing your teeth every morning.

Most people, like 90% of them, need just 6 months to see visible progress in whatever skill they are learning. If you don't see visible progress in 6 months you are definitely doing something wrong. If you follow everything written in this book you would probably see visible progress even faster than that at around 4 months. 6 months is just 0.007% of your life considering you live till 70. What I am saying is that 0.007% if done well can be life altering.

TIME IS KING

Time is Money; we have all heard this, but actually, time is worth way more than money. Ask a billionaire on her deathbed, and she will tell you that she would pay anything for another gasp of life. I could simply end this chapter by saying don't waste your time and be productive, but you already know that and so do I. What we also know is that no matter how much we try, we somehow end up watching a movie or just letting our minds wander off while we try to truly put our heads into something. Don't our idols get distracted? How on earth are they so laser-focused? Well, the truth is they aren't. First of all, stop thinking of people who are good at something as these godly beings who made it despite all obstacles. The only reason they made it was because of their obstacles, and without them, they would be right where you are standing today (AVERAGE).

Even if they goofed off just like you, they did some things differently that made them better, since we all are humans with a perfectly functioning brain I think we all have the ability to achieve the stuff our idols achieved. How long it takes may vary, but we can all certainly get there. Here are some facts you need to hear.

- Everyone has problems: the rich, the poor and everyone in between.

- Everyone has some sort of ambition, even if it's deep inside them, and some digging needs to be done.

- Everyone has the same time, the same days, and depending on where you are from, more or less the same amount of years to live. In fact, even people who died way younger than you have also made a dent on this world.

- Average is a choice, and we let life choose for us instead of choosing our life.

Time has everything to do with your perspective on life. Those 4 hours you spend on your phone every day will add up to 11 years of your lifetime, assuming you live till 75. 11 years are more than enough to become a professional at anything you want. If you want to be above average, change your perspective on time. Ordinary people always think they have a lot of time on their hands, but the truth is we don't. Do you know why children are able to learn faster than adults? It's because they know how to strip away the inessentials. Children don't have any responsibilities, fear of failure, or lack of attention. All they need is a bit of encouragement, and they would literally dedicate hours of their time each day to working on the things they are curious about. As adults, we lose that curiosity, and our motivation becomes corrupt. We start learning for money or fame or to impress our crush. That is why it is all the more disappointing when we realise that we suck at the things we learn and give up.

We need to learn for the sake of learning and let time do its magic. If you do something long enough, no matter how bad you are at it in the beginning, you will definitely get better with time. The only problem is that the longer you do something, the more your curiosity or passion for it slowly starts to dwindle. Now, I am not saying that your passion for it will die; you will still enjoy it, but the curious flame within you will slowly start to extinguish. The only way to prevent this is by finally being brave enough to bring your ideas to life. At this point, you would clearly have the skills to do that, but you will still need a push to truly believe that you are finally capable enough to venture into and find your own style. Years of failing, humiliation, and self-doubt will make this decision really hard, but you will have a choice: either let the flame die out or start a fire with the beautiful mind you have.

Life is too short, and time is king. It may seem enough, but trust me, once you start to create and implement your learning, it will never be enough. All the greats like Elvis, Tesla, and countless others wished for the thing that you possess and squander away, "Time". According to some studies, the human brain has around 50,000 to 70,000 thoughts a day. Imagine how many great ideas form during that time. No matter how many of those ideas we act upon, we will never have enough time to do it all.

But anytime is a good time. Think of it this way: you are at the worst moment in your life; you feel terrible and have nothing to look forward to, but then you start learning something new with no real goal in mind. It still brings a brink of positivity into your life. Now you have a reason to get up in the morning and get out of the rock bottom you have been eternally stuck in. We can also flip the coin: you have a great life. The dream life, if you may call it. You decide to learn something new just to experiment with yourself and explore who you are. In both these cases, you are learning for the sake of learning, which is the most important thing you can do. In the first case, you are learning because you literally have nothing to lose, and in the second case, you are learning to grow and branch out your roots. These are intrinsic motivators that come from within you and are far better than extrinsic motivators like money. The biggest difference is that intrinsic motivation teaches you to accept failure while extrinsic motivation makes you avoid it as much as possible, and as I have told you before, failure is always going to be your best teacher while learning something new.

Let me end this chapter by telling you a little secret I have come to know with the help of countless observations I have made about myself and others

- You need just 6 months to be Above Average at something

- You need just 2 years to be Good at something

- You need just 5 years to be Amazing at something

That is the biggest cheat code to learning something. Anything, for that matter. So it's irrelevant when you start. This is literally all you need. Of course, you have to follow all the steps you read about in this book, but when you do. You can see the results. Getting good at something is seriously over-exaggerated in our heads. It's honestly not as hard as we think it is. The 10,000 hours thing may be true, but honestly, we don't need that much time; we don't need to be masters at our craft. We just need to be good enough to get our ideas out to the world.

FOCUS ON THE FEW

Do you know how you can be happy when there is chaos all around you? It's by focusing on the few good things that actually happen around you. Even a bad day has something good hidden in it. Just try looking. When you learn something new, you will most definitely have more bad days than good. So treat every day as a good day because you were bold enough to try.

Now, as your learning journey continues and you pick up the new skills you always wanted to learn, people will start to know you as that guy who is good at (your skills). It feels good. Now, you have to make one of the toughest decisions of your life. This decision will most definitely be painstaking but life altering. YOU have to DECIDE to PRIORITIZE. Remember how, at the start of the book, I told you doing one skill can be very monotonous. Unfortunately, we can't run away from that monotony forever. The first half of the book was meant for you to try as many new things as you could and realise that you could actually be good at them all. That open-mindedness has got you reading this far.

But from this point forward, we are going to break the cycle. We are going to become liberated from the average life. This is when the path to mastery really begins. It's a hard path indeed, a path of uncertainty. That is why it was my moral duty to show you that even if this path doesn't work, you can find another calling. So it is what I call going all in without really risking anything. From this interjection, this book will be more directed towards mastery or, rather, getting your ideas together. Well, the truth is no matter what you do, the world often disappoints. Even if you make the best song or the best YouTube video or write the best fucking piece of litterateur, the world always disappoints. Things will never ever go according to plan, so we have to be strategic because we literally have to fight the world to win.

So here is what I suggest

1. Have Two Skills That Would Make You Money

2. Have One Skill That You would Do For Free even If it meant you would never make any money from it

Now, more often than not, the latter would probably make you a ton of money in the long run, but it is also the skill that will disappoint you the most. The skills that make you money would be less fun to do, and that frustration of not getting enough time for your passion would paradoxically motivate you to do more in the skill you are learning for your intrinsic satisfaction. Fortunately or unfortunately, money has everything to do with how much better you can get in the skills you learn. This is because the less you have to worry about money, the more time and resources you can spend learning what you like. So, the learning problem is also a money problem.

How To Find Your Calling

Finding your calling is the most overrated thing ever. It is as simple as sticking to things for as long as you possibly can. Out of all the skills we want to learn, we will have to stick to only one or a maximum of two skills for 4 to 5 years. All the other skills we can learn and keep in our arsenal. But around 6 months to a year of training would be fine for that. The reason to focus on a few has nothing to do with our ability to learn. As I have proved earlier on multiple occasions, we can learn whatever the fuck we want and even get pretty good at it. The actual reason for eventually focusing on a few skills is because of our lack of enough money and time on our hands. We can make more money at some point, but we can never buy lost time.

So I want you to take a journal and write the list of skills you have learned till now and you are "above average" at. Now, I really want you to think about those skills which you can actually stick with for 4 to 5 years. You will definitely find skills that you won't be able to stick with for so long on your list. For me, those skills are boxing and chess. No doubt I am above average at chess now, and I am proud of that. I know that someday soon, I will be above average at boxing, too. These are the facts I have come to terms with while also realising that I would not want to pursue these skills for 4 to 5 years because my goals do not match these fields of interest as much. For you, it will obviously be different things, but writing it down and really being introspective helps. You will be able to clearly differentiate between the skills you want to learn just because you want to be decent at it and the skills you want to learn that you want to be fucking amazing at.

Now, further Segregate those skills into earners and intrinsic skills.

Once you get a more wholesome picture, you have to actually calculate its financial aspect.

Learning something and deciding to be fucking amazing does not come cheap but think of it as investing in yourself. People who decide that they do not want to be average heavily invest in themselves. I want you to create an Excel sheet calculating approximately how much you will be spending in the next 3 years to actually learn the skills you would like to learn, as well as calculate the total hours you will be learning just with the help of the coach. Spoiler alert: that amount would be huge but know that 3 years of learning that skill will be enough to turn your ideas into reality, and that is the goal, isn't it? Personally, my guitar classes for 3 years would cost me around Rs.64,800, that is just Rs.1800 a month, mind you, and my singing class would cost me around Rs.1,08,000 with hours of training 216 hrs and 72 hrs, respectively. Now, you must have glanced at the numbers and thought to yourself, is that even worth it? I want you to know that these hours spent are mostly for feedback and learning new concepts. Your true training is done during your practice hours, which are free. So we can add another 300 hours to each. Just by creating that one Excel sheet, I made it real and got a much broader and precise picture of exactly where I would stand. Now I have never really believed in the 10,000-hour bullshit, especially in this generation where nobody has time for anything.

So personally I am content spending these many hours on the skills I learn. Maybe after 3 years I would get bored or maybe I might just give up after 2 but I would at least know where I am going.

It's ok to be unsure of the stuff you do. Now, we don't know if there is a pot of gold waiting for us on the other side, but what we do know is that learning new things makes us feel good about ourselves. It's alright and normal to question our choices while we are on this journey. Even I find myself questioning and wondering sometimes if it is even worth it to write this book. Truth be told, I have wanted to give up more than once, but it's just that I have come so far that I can't stop now. I have never come this far in writing before, and the fact that I have shown that this book means something to me is irrelevant to the results. Sometimes, working on something for way too long also forces us to keep going no matter how we feel about the thing we are learning; we just keep coming back to it. Determination is just the fear of losing your progress.

Callings and Goals

"Don't set goals. Set ridiculously small goals". We have all heard that saying. Well, the opposite is also true from what I have realised. Setting ridiculously big goals also works sometimes. Just like I did with this book. My goal was to finish writing 50 pages of this book by the end of the year. It seemed easy and all, but 10 months went by without really achieving much. Now I could either say to myself it's ok there is always next year or say fuck that, I need to do this no matter what. So I have just around two months left to write 20 pages and achieve what I initially set out to achieve, and I thought it would be super easy. Well, most of my time went into observing life from a broader perspective to write shit that's actually meaningful, and the rest of my time went into slacking off. There is this beautiful theory called Parkinson's Law.

It says, " Work Expands To Fill The Time Allotted To Its Completion". So, it basically means that we will slack off at every opportunity we can get and don't really need as much time as we think to do a particular task. So I say: Set those ridiculously big goals because the truth is if you actually try, you can achieve them very well. Don't change your goals to fit your convenience because that would just make it much harder to actually follow through. Now, I could tell you that writing 50 pages could very well take me a decade if I keep telling myself, "I need to research more", but at the end of the day, I can always come back to what I wrote instead of looking at a blank sheet of paper.

DEMENTORS

So my girlfriend recently showed me the "Harry Potter Movies". Yes, I had never seen Harry Potter before. I was too scared of Dobby as a kid. Why am I telling you this? It's because Harry Potter and "The Real World" have one thing in common: Dementors. For all you non-Harry Potter watchers over here, first of all, go watch it, and second of all, Dementors are a sort of soul-sucking beings who thrive on killing other people's joy. Our world has more Dementors than Azkaban. People who don't understand talent will criticise anything and everything just to make themselves feel better. They would joke about how you suck so much at something and should quit altogether.

For me, my Dementors have been my parents and a few classmates here and there. Remember, people who care about you would never say that. There is a huge difference between criticism and constructive criticism. We need to really know our support systems, who is really on our side, and who is being pretentious.

Example:

1. Why are you still doing this? Get a real job, and stop wasting your time.

2. Hey, you're not good at it, but I believe in you, and you will improve.

Tell me how reading both these statements feels. The first one just puts you in a bad mood. The second one acknowledges that you aren't quite there yet but says that it's okay and that you will eventually get there. Both have the same core message but yet are poles apart. One makes you feel like you are completely useless, while the other gives you the positive energy and confidence you need to persevere in the skill you are trying to learn. General advice could be "STAY AWAY FROM Dementors", but honestly, our world is filled with so many of them that you really can't avoid them all together. They will try to hurt you in every way they can, so what you need is a shield.

Finding Your Shield

All you need is just 2 people believing in you. Why 2 instead of one? That's because our brain is very good at receiving negative signals but sucks at taking positive signals. If someone says you will never be good enough. You instantly believe them without ever questioning it, but when someone says you are going to be good at it. You will question their judgement in every way possible. Is that person just saying it as a friend? Can they really see something I don't see? What about the others who hate what I am doing? "YOU ARE YOUR BIGGEST FAN" You need to get this straight through your head. The second person is you, yourself. Whenever you get attacked by a dementor, you need to go and talk to the person who believes in you, but after that is the most important part. You need to introspect and take their belief and add it to your own belief. Confident people aren't born. They are made. This shield of positive affirmations is literally the only thing you need to fall in love with the journey. If you love the journey, you will get better with time.

Victim Culture and The Imposter Syndrome

If you learn anything at all from this book, I want you to learn this. So listen up closely. **WE CAN MAKE IT HAPPEN IF WE STOP BEING THE VICTIM.** I have never lost an opportunity to blame my parents for my life up until recently when I realised. Yes, they fucked up, but I still have to deal with the consequences. Being the victim was simply not good enough for me anymore. If I let the world write my story, it will surely do it. It would set its so-called realistic dreams upon me. Wife, Kids, one vacation a year, work until you jump off a five-story building. I took responsibility for my own actions just recently. Did the shit I wanted to despite what the world said. You are wasting your time. Use your money on better things, ya da… This new version of me also found myself in a new problem. I was in a quandary. It was finally happening, taking charge of my life. I started to have what is commonly known as the imposter syndrome. This is when you think you will never be good enough even though you are better than most people. It sucks when you are trying something new, and Dementors are always ready to judge you. You might also start being a dementor if you let victimisation and the imposter syndrome rule your world. Now, there isn't much you can do about it except positive affirmations and letting time pass. The truth is if you stick long enough to something, you will get there. How long is not the question, but rather, how do I stick long?

Satisfaction isn't in pleasing others but in pleasing yourself

STOP THINKING

We humans are gifted with a big functioning brain that is honestly the best of any species. It can also be a curse sometimes when you have to make a conscious effort for every little thing you desire. Why can't it be an urge like masturbating? or Eating or Sleeping? We do all these things religiously and can't survive too long without them. Why can't we turn the things we want to learn into urges of ours? Things we can simply not survive without.

Why can't we turn learning into something as addictive as Instagram? The only reason behind this is that when we learn something new, we create new neural pathways, which can only be done with a conscious mind. Only once those pathways are created and strong will an urge to do that thing generate. That is what we humans call passion, but it is just the urge caused by intense stimulation our brain gives us when we do something well. It can take decades to do so, but once you get there, you simply stop thinking too consciously, and the subconscious takes over. The subconscious can do things that our conscious mind can simply never replicate.

It is where all the great ideas come to life. We can improve upon them consciously, but only subconsciously can we form them vaguely in our heads. When we turn something we learn into an urge, it leads to more practice and, therefore, more improvement.

But, like always, there needs to be a method to this madness, and it needs to be intrinsic. So, the question lies before us: how can we turn learning into an urge?

Well, for starters, we can start associating it with something we already like. For example, I love the spotlight and the stage, and music has become my medium to shine on the stage. Similarly, I associate chess and boxing with physical and mental fitness. I find it thrilling to talk and socialise with new people, so sometimes I learn to socialise and connect. Of course, you will have your own enticements that induce you.

Bonus Points

When I started writing this book, I started my learning journey. Something I realised now that I didn't back then are the bonus points. When you pick something to learn, you are actually learning way more than you originally intended. These extra things are either learned by you to get better at your original skill or just picked up subconsciously. We often turn a blind eye to these bonus points. In my case with boxing, I finally learned something I always wanted to but didn't know how, and that was skipping. With graphic design, I learned how to play with colours and tell what goes with what. Indirectly improved my fashion sense.

Now that I know learning gives me bonus points while simultaneously developing my personality, I am twice as motivated to do what I do. Knowing these small things can really trick your brain into working hard and being consistent. It has surely helped me come a long way. I hope it does the same for you.

Write down the skills you are learning and also the temptations you want to use to keep learning these skills. (It could be anything I can't Judge)

Skills			
Temptations			

After you fill this table I want you to take a picture of it and see it on the days you don't feel like doing something. Spoiler alert we are going to talk about that next.

Down Days and The Guilt

An unexpected thing that comes with learning is guilt and mental pressure. Think of it as a mould that first pushes against you to make you stronger. I am not going to lie. There have been days when I was depressed that I was not doing enough or not improving and questioned everything. The progress you see on social media and the sheer talent some people possess make almost everything you do seem futile. The pressure of learning something new is that you will question its worthiness in your life every time you feel down. Some days, when it gets too stressful or I feel I can't take this pressure, I take a step back and reward myself with a rest day. Now you must be thinking, how can I really tell the difference between burnout and just laziness? Well, the main difference is burnout comes and hits you on random days, and it usually occurs after a few months of learning something. Laziness can be pushed through, but pushing through burnout isn't the wisest idea. You might push through in the short run, but in the long run, you will simply lose that spark of learning, and it will start to feel like a chore.

Life is going to be hard. It is always going to get in the way. We are always going to be emotional creatures. That's why our goal isn't to train hard but rather to train a medium amount over extended periods of time. Bad days will come, and rest is equally important as actively trying to learn something. Pushing yourself is okay, but pushing yourself while losing the essence of life may not be the best idea. Big changes occur only with time, and that's okay. Even if you practised every single day for 5 hours straight for a whole month, you still wouldn't be as good as someone who practised 1 hour a day for five months because our brain takes time to register information. Five months of practice, despite the practice being of the same time span, is more effective, at least in my point of view. This is mainly because you simply cannot generate enough motivation to push yourself 5 hours a day for a month while sacrificing most things in your life. Only a handful of us can achieve the first one, so it would be better if we focused on the latter.

The days when you skip learning or just can't convince yourself to even do 5 minutes of it. You are going to feel guilt. You can either frown and over-scrutinise your decision, or you can enjoy a day of rest knowing that you will catch up. The reason you didn't do what you were supposed to on that particular day could be endless. Not getting enough sleep or work or literally anything might come up in this unpredictable life. I used to feel guilty and become sad that I was not doing enough instead of knowing that I was doing as much as I could. We all have our limits on how much we can learn in a day, but what we can control as individuals is to decide to stick with it even if we skip a few days here and there. Don't let this become a habit, though, or laziness will take over. So, for every reason not to do something, you should at least have two reasons for doing it. This is because you voluntarily decided to learn this skill. Nobody forced you into it, not your parents, not your friends, not your boss, but you. So that means you desire to one day be good at that skill, and therefore, you must not run away from putting in the work to get there. We all have the map, and we all have some resources to get there as well; all we need to do is walk towards the treasure.

Self Learning Resources

In today's generation, I honestly think Chat GPT is a better learning source than Google. It has an unfathomable amount of data and knowledge that it can explain to you in the simplest terms if you ask it to. Earlier information was hard to comprehend depending on the depth of research you did, but now all of that complex jargon can be simplified such that even a child with a basic reading ability can understand.

Besides that, of course, YouTube tutorials are always helpful because people make tutorials for everything under the sun. But these can sometimes be misleading due to the abundance of information. People may also have different opinions on different concepts or might explain in different ways. Sometimes, YouTube can give you the best advice, and other times, the worst. So be careful

The most effective way to learn something, though, is always going to be through books and reading. For all nonreaders like me, you can use audiobooks. The only reason I recommend books is because books have to surpass the quality check of publishers, and only after the approval of the publishers are they sent to the public. Also, usually, a single book explores the topic in such a way that a beginner can inchmeal go on a journey with the author.

Paid Courses are another great option and are better than going on an unstructured route. They will give you a sense of direction and some courses also have communities you can join along with them to share your learning progress and be accountable.

LOOK BACK

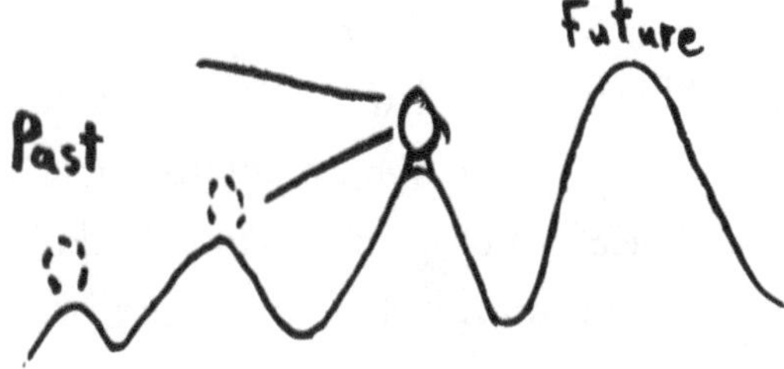

All that self-shame and self-critique from the time you started learning the skill you wanted to master has to be put behind you. I want you to remember all those people who judged you, all the Dementors, as how terrible you were. Oftentimes, we forget to look back, and that creates self-shame, which is ludicrous and has nothing to do with reality. You will never be as bad as you were a month ago. Even if you can't see it, slowly, everyone around you starts to notice except yourself. In your head, you are still the worst, but the naked truth is that you have progressed. This is the main reason why looking back is important. Keep your old works with you no matter how bad they were so that you have something to compare with. The only fight you have is with yourself.

When I heard my voice from 6 months ago, I could tell each and every mistake I made, and at that time, I thought what I did was pretty good. It doesn't mean the past version of me was wrong, but rather that the "past me" had not explored the knowledge of the present version of me. Although I am not good yet, I know I am better, and I also know that I will get there someday, but that also means that I don't want to spend all my life hating my voice. If I chose not to look back, I would still think I have not improved at all because your mind can deceive you. Also, some days, you have good days, but most days are going to be bad.

Being self-aware of your true skills instead of your perceived skills can really boost your confidence. My mantra is when you're bad at something, try thinking you are average and work on it, and when you become good, don't be too hard on yourself because there will never be a version of you that will be good enough if you don't let it. There will be a point where you are good at something but also have your own unique style at the skill you do. Some people may love it, and some may hate it, but that doesn't really define your true ability.

John Callahan was a paralysed American cartoonist. He made comics because it gave him joy. If you read his comics, you will either find them offensive or funny; there is no in between. He brought out a strong emotion in people. Not all were positive, but not all were negative either. Does that mean he was a bad comic artist? It doesn't matter what we believe. It only matters what he believed. We are only as good or bad as we believe we are.

If you asked him to look back at his life. It was a fucking mess filled with alcoholism and depression. He still had to look back and accept his life as it was just like you have to look back and accept how you were at learning something in the past, but that will never mean you are still like that. So believe in yourself, and you will feel powerful in your work.

Two days ago, my 21st Birthday passed. Yay, Happy Birthday to Me!!! However, I also took this opportunity to reflect on the actions of the 20-year-old me, and I saw a huge change both emotionally and physically. When I looked back, I realised that I had achieved some things I never thought I was ready to achieve, but my skills sufficed. I think our reality is the one we create, not what the world hands us. The changes we implement in life won't be visible now, but a year, 2 years, 5 years down the line, you will find that your life turned out well and compounding is doing a great job with your life. It's not how much you do, but rather how long you do it, that turns you from zero to hero.

Try Writing a Few Changes You Observed since Your Last Birthday

Looking back doesn't solely mean looking at your past, though. You can also look back from a future perspective. I want you to close your eyes and imagine. Imagine how you are on the stage in your first tournament or in your rose garden that you finally learned to maintain. The things we desire to learn can be anything, but it's important to fantasise about them and put ourselves in those shoes. Make your fantasy a reality by thinking about the details. Like when I imagine myself singing, I imagine what my voice would sound like in the future based on what it sounds like right now; when I imagine myself playing the guitar, I imagine the style I am playing. Visualisation brings you closer to where you want to be because you know that those people in your head are just versions of yourself you have yet to unlock, so it feels more achievable the more concrete your vision is.

THE BEST MISTAKES

All our lives, we have been told to stay the fuck away from mistakes. Our school, our home, and our work keep reiterating it. We start something new, and everyone thinks it's a mistake. We, as humans, have evolved to despise change in any shape or form. It doesn't matter how much it's hurting us. We would rather choose pain over progress. That is the simple reason why people keep bitching about their jobs but never actually do anything about it, even though action isn't that hard in this era.

Honestly, whoever has been bold enough to make these "mistakes" looks back at them and calls it a life-defining moment. That is what they become because they get us out of our comfort zone, and that is when our survival instincts kick in. Instead of feeling guilty about trying new things, instead of making excuses next time, think that maybe one of these mistakes might turn into your best mistake. I won't lie; it will take a lot of courage to make these mistakes, and society will never accept you, but ignore society for once, and you will see what a wonderful feeling it is to try out new things. Our mistakes bring us more growth than our successes, so why not embrace them with open arms? In life, nobody really knows what they are doing, so in somebody's eyes, you will always be making a huge mistake. So, does it really matter? No, it does not. When you discover that you can live for yourself and not just for others, you get to truly explore yourself and find the answer to questions like your purpose, the meaning of life to you, and whatnot. Learning new things should excite you, and if you care about something, nobody else has to.

Sometimes, opportunities knock on your door, even when other people call them mistakes. On my 18th birthday, I decided to start investing in the stock market when covid had hit. Everyone called it the worst time to start investing, which is a big mistake, according to them. Fast forward 2 years later, those same stocks made over 60% returns. I saw what others didn't. I saw panic, which was temporary. People thrive on negativity, so when the world is a pessimist, you need to be an optimist. Now people look at me and say I got lucky. I believe **Luck = Strong Belief + Hard Work**. I remember watching a lot of YouTube videos to understand how the stock market actually worked, and now I can confidently say it has come to work out in my favour.

Right now, my friends say I am making a big mistake in learning everything at once. Little do they know that I have thought long and hard about how I can achieve this and am documenting everything in this book. I am confident that my learning theories won't disappoint even if people think it's a mistake to spend so much time learning instead of partying or hanging out with friends. Hanging out doesn't take much effort, but learning can be a bittersweet journey, so why not do it when you are young and have all the energy, fewer responsibilities, and more time in your hands? Well, this in no way means that you can't learn when you are older. What I am trying to say is never have the fear of missing out because, in all honesty, when you love learning and know that here is where you want to be, you are not missing out on anything.

The Biggest and Best mistake you can make is just being a little courageous sometimes. A few moments of courage now and then will surprise you with the changes it can bring to your life. Being bold and stupid are different things, though. Know the difference. Being bold is when you want something and believe in something, but the world thinks it's a bad idea, and being stupid is when you want something just because you were told it's a bad idea. Believe first and only then pursue. People say being **'Naive'** is a big mistake, but I say we all need to be a little naive at the start. We can't all always have a plan from start to finish; sometimes, we just need to see where it goes. If it goes well, that's a win for us, but if it doesn't, we will still be decent at it even if we decide to drop it later.

Make more mistakes because the more you fuck around, the faster you learn what not to do. I came to realise something about learning recently. That is the power of self-realisation. Even when my instructors tell me I am doing something wrong, nothing changes until I realise my mistake on my own. Sometimes, I get there faster with their feedback, but sometimes, it takes a while to actually comprehend and self-realise what they mean. This realisation only comes after making the same mistake so many times that my brain just automatically comes up with a better solution to the problem. An instructor can only identify your mistakes and let you know about them, but it is only you who can implement their suggestions gradually over time.

Scrutiny and Self Destruction

Maybe I am not good enough? Why is everyone so ahead of me? Worth it? Why don't I do the things my parents think are right for me? Fuck those thoughts. When you make mistakes, you will feel like shit, and when you feel like shit, you will scrutinise yourself. The doubtful path is always a destructive one. Don't lead yourself into self-destruction by constantly doubting yourself. I am only telling you this because I do that too, but I also know that this is only a phase where you are getting towards being good at something but aren't quite there yet. This phase can last a couple of months or even years, but I can guarantee you that it won't last more than five years. Once you do something for that long, you get used to it, and when you get used to it, you will stop feeling shit about yourself. However, ability only, along with confidence in your ability, can get you there. Think that this shall come to pass whenever you get dark thoughts and feel like quitting. The only reason you are compelled to quit is because today's world is fast-paced. Nobody wants to spend so long perfecting their crafts. It also doesn't help to know that AI can replace you anytime in any fucking field.

That is why I talk about beating the average at something in this book because once you get there you can finally do what AI can't. That is, be original in your fucking thoughts.

Troubled Times and Failures

Failure is the stepping stone to success; we all have heard this saying, but do you really know what it means? It means that each time you spectacularly fail at something, you are not at rock bottom but a step above it. It is what I call the compounding failure effect. Your failures compound either one of two ways according to how you think. It either breaks your morale, slowly decays your dreams and aspirations, or compounds your learning due to your mistakes, and each time you fail, you are one step closer to where you want to be. Restart because each time you do, you aren't starting from scratch but rather have a new perspective on how to get there. A very unconventional approach to faster learning is when it's your only way out. Yes, you heard that right. People learn much quicker when they are royally screwed if they don't get to where they want to. Now, believe me when I say this is an extreme case, and most of us won't ever be required to use this method, but when learning the skill becomes our last resort, a do-or-die situation, we learn and actually get good at the thing we are learning much quicker.

I just happen to be lucky enough to be in a situation where I am royally screwed. So, I will study this approach firsthand and tell you more about it. Next year, I have to move out whatsoever, and I am scared. But when you are the most afraid, it is the time for drastic change. To help "you fellow readers" out, you can try a very effective alternative to trauma. It's called consequential learning. Automate the consequences, and you will always do your best. What the fuck do I mean by automate the consequences?. This concept can be a little perplexing at first, but it is an easy way to change your perspective on the urgency of the situation.

So, I want you to take a notebook and write the words "**consequences of not learning this skill**".

Then list out at least 4 consequences on the page. Now I want you to write down the exaggerated or extreme version of what would happen if you don't learn that skill.

For Example The consequences of not learning chess. I might get slower, It may reduce my strategy abilities. I won't have a medium to let out my stress, It will reduce my time management abilities.

The Exaggerated Version: I might forget how to play the game completely, I may lose my ability to think under pressure, the stress in me will build up and might lead to anxiety, I will be bad at managing my time and it will reduce my efficiency.

The second version seems a lot more alarming, doesn't it? Stick it on your cupboard, fridge, or someplace you can look at it daily. One thing you have to keep in mind is to try this with only one skill at a time, or else it will defeat the urgency perceived. After you do it, I want you to just have a glance at it every two or three days or on the days you think you should give up. Giving this a quick glance will create motivation and also help build discipline. We don't truly push ourselves until it is our last choice.

If you have made it this far into the book and actually bothered to try out the advice given here. You must have definitely started to see some concrete changes in your life. I want you to write them down in the table below.

What Changes have you started to observe
in your life?

FIRE DIES

Small changes lead to big ones, but how do you keep reminding yourself that in a world where everyone wants everything quickly? We want the sex but not the time and effort to build a meaningful connection, we want money but don't have the patience to build and fail at business, and we want to master new skills, but it seems to take fucking forever to get there. Do we even have it in us?

Motivation is a myth. The idea that people who succeed have the most motivation is the most bullshit thing we are made to believe. If we were given good money, decent sex, and decent food. Nobody would ever give a fuck about wanting something more. Another thing that is a myth is passion. Passion is a love-hate relationship. You can be passionate about something and also hate doing it at times. There will always be stuff we like about the process and stuff we hate doing. Like, I love playing music and original songs, but I hate having to think about how to improve, practice, and master them. Now, the question that sits across the table is, do we just skip the stuff we hate? The obvious answer is no. But what if we could put on a facade and fool ourselves into enjoying it? When the fire dies, relight it with the candle of dreams.

I think the trick to solving this puzzle is the rule of 3\4th. Whenever you are working on something new and creating something, For every 3 out of 4 things you create, do it with all your passion, and on the 4th project, just have fun and mess around. This will develop instinct, which will eventually lead to effortless learning or, as I call it, learning on autopilot. Another trick I follow is to do what I hate first and then move on to the parts that I love doing. Giving your brain hope and something pleasant to look forward to in the short run will boost your willpower immensely.

Well, earlier, I told you that passion fades away, but most of us aren't even sure what passion is. Passion is the excitement we get when we are learning something or working on a personal project in sync with those skills. So, theoretically, if you can get yourself excited about something, you can most definitely feel passion for it. Our brain loves giving signals to our body, and the more happy signals we can get, such as dopamine, adrenaline, and other chemicals, the more motivation we get. Adrenaline just happens to be an easy chemical to release. Just put yourself in places you usually don't hang around, and you will achieve adrenaline. For example, if you are learning cycling, go off-roading sometimes, or if you are learning to cook, then find people to taste it and give you a scorecard. These little changes will always keep you motivated and help reignite your fire.

To feel excited about the things you learn, you can also dabble in some gamification. Try turning the process into mini-games and reward yourself at each level. This way, even the most boring days will turn into " I want to win this game I created". For singing, according to how many warm-ups I do, I give myself points. Writing my own song gets extra points.

Keep it Challenging

We do not give our best when there is one of 2 things: either the task is way too hard for us to grasp, or it is way too easy to end up boring us. What we need is a balance. When I got a fracture and had to leave my 1 and half years of weight training behind me to recover and join boxing for a while. I knew what I was going to lose. I lost most of my muscles, and when I recently went back to the gym, I was just a shadow of my former self. So, instead of the dread of losing it all, I took it in a positive way and turned my passion for the gym into a challenge. I have given myself 6 months to reach my former capabilities, and I very well know I can reach there. So sometimes, when you retouch a skill after a long time (4 months in my case), then always keep this in mind: "If you can do it once, you can do it again." Many people don't talk about relearning skills. Since learning isn't really in our biology, and we literally have to break neural links to learn new skills, it is obvious that some paths will disconnect, and that's why relearning is as important as learning. The right amount of challenge and the right plan to get there are all you need when you feel the fire is dying. These things will rekindle the joy you have for learning the skill.

Game Plan

Planning comes second nature to us humans. Our brains can be rewired to think about long-term outcomes rather than just short-term. This skill is unique to us, and we need to exploit it while learning. This is called Delayed Gratification. All this sounds good in theory, but without knowing how to practically implement these theories, it is all bullshit. So, I am going to focus on the practical implementation because you don't intend to give an exam on this topic. So get your pen and fill in the following things in the table.

Where You Stand	Where You Want To Stand	Reason to Get There	How To Get There

When your passion starts to dwindle, you need to make a plan to push yourself to the next level. Knowing where you stand is the first step. Only the conscious mind can make an effort to change. The next thing to think about is where you want to stand. When things get boring, setting a fresh goal is what keeps us going. All this won't be possible without a strong reason, though. Motivation comes from vision, so find your reasons.

Once you are clear on all three reasons, I am going to help you figure out the most important thing on the table.

How To Get There?

The most effective way to figure out how to get there is to simply follow the 20 rule. Take a notebook and list out 20 ways to get where you want to get. Try to be very specific with what you write. This won't come easy. The first 4 or 5 ways will be easy but as you think harder you will come up with clear and realistic ways to get to your goal and by the time you hit the 20th way. You will find your answer.

Obviously, at this stage, we can't work on all the skills with this intensity, so pick one. We are now officially better than most people in all the skills we started to learn from the start of this book. Now, It's time to go from above average to good. For me, the skills I have removed at this stage are chess and boxing. So, I want to focus on Singing, Guitar, and Graphic design. These skills could be totally different for you; it is just trying to think of which skills actually have a future in your life and which you want to pursue as a hobby.

TEACHING IS THE BEST TEACHER

Once you are above average you are ready to be a teacher. Yes, you can actually teach what you learned now. Obviously, you are at no stage to make money from it yet but try teaching to get something more valuable than money, a strong network. Teaching teaches you to express your ideas as well as to revisit old concepts.

I personally took up the challenge to teach people something I am above average at, and that is public speaking. I was never a natural public speaker, but over time, I built my skills to make myself above average. The first-ever public speaking class I took as a teacher had just one student, but now I have managed to build it slowly and am proud to say I have 6 students under my belt. Working on something much bigger than you will help you push your limits just like it helped push mine. Is it going to be easy? Fuck No. Honestly, some days, you would wish that you were better off without it; push through those days as this journey will unlock a perspective that you can never see merely as a student.

Teaching is a demanding job, and the anxiety of conveying your ideas the right way can often leave you distraught. I remember my heart beating and my mind becoming foggy due to the stress of not being good enough. Well, the truth is that being good takes time, and working on conveying your ideas is where the magic happens. The thing is, when you start teaching, you begin to explore the subject deeper just so that you can share your findings with your students. This not only helps you relearn but also makes you realise the limitless possibilities. Your experiences can only take you so far; true mastery occurs when you learn from others' experiences.

If you don't seem like the teaching type, maybe you can be the problem-solver type. This is where you get to help people who need your skills for free. Show them what you can do for them. How does that help you? You let people know that you are available for work and can explore your talents and show them. While doing this, though, always be careful to show it to the right people. The world is filled with exploiters, and if you aren't careful, you won't really be able to help someone who genuinely appreciates your skill. Once you are good enough, finding people you can help is a must, as it will increase your confidence, as well as their confidence in you.

The whole point of either teaching or helping people out is to get a feedback loop running from within. The more you teach, the more you explore different types of scenarios and how to deal with real-life problems within the skill you are learning. The goal is to understand the skill you want to be good at even deeper than you began with. Now, you are better than most people but still not the best or relatively good. Teaching and helping people will let you test yourself and push your skills to the limit to expand your horizon of thinking.

What You Want to Teach	People you taught

This table will help you keep track or at least give you a starting line where you can write down the exact skill you intend to teach and go ahead with helping beginners learn.

Give value to the right person, and you will get value back.

THE ROAD NOT TAKEN

So today was a big fucking step in my life. "I just dropped out of college the second time". Honestly, I am scared about where to go next, but the stuff I was studying in college was not taking me there. Uncertainty is a painful journey. Maybe someday, this decision will prove worth it, but I have no way of knowing right now.

Oftentimes in life, we have 2 roads, and we need to choose one while letting go of the other completely.

The road we take is our choice, but the consequences we face are not our choice. The same is true with your skills; if you followed the things mentioned in this book, you definitely crossed the average threshold. Now, the choice is yours to double down on the things that mean the most to you. We have one life, and while we can be better than everyone else at most things with time, effort, and practice, mastery is a whole new ball game. A single person can only be great at a handful of skills, and that is something we need to be okay with. Being great requires us to let go of the other skills and accept that we can only go so far at them. We don't have to quit, but we need to prioritize our most important skills, where we don't want to be good but the best at our game. From the beginning of this book, I made it very clear that this book will help you go from bad to above average or even good if you try to be consistent at it, but being great at something is a different path from here. It is not a cycle of changing things but rather a constant urge to do something.

Well, most of you would probably never face such a tough decision in life where it is a do-or-die situation, but that doesn't mean you shouldn't double down. Up until this point, you must have become the jack of all trades, but now the book will talk about mastering one.

The first thing that you need to realise before trying to master something is that you won't be able to make up your mind about what you want to master. So here are some points to keep in mind. Does time pass by in an instant sometimes when you are working on that skill? Are you excited and planning how you are going to execute or practice? Do other people think you are good at it? And finally, does it make you feel like you are making a difference?

Only if you are able to say yes to all of these questions will you find your thing to double down on. The skill you have found might be glamorous, like acting, singing, or sports, or might be less recognised, like cooking, photography, or chess. Unfortunately, we can only choose to improve ourselves in the fields we like, but the skill we want to master more or less chooses us rather than the other way around. It doesn't mean you have to give up on everything else. It just means you will need to give most of your time here.

Trust is a very big part of mastering a skill. If you don't trust yourself, the journey gets ten times harder because I can assure you that nobody will. The world disappoints, and it's true. It always has. The people who care about you the most will also fail to see what you see. Oftentimes, believing we can be the best is a hard pill to swallow because you will hear countless times that you aren't good enough, others are better than you, and you need a backup plan. The thing about backup plans is that they never are the life we dream of; they are the life we get if we fail. Having some fear of failure is the only route to success. Imagine if it wasn't stressful and you knew that you had something to fall back on. Would it work out for you? Probably not. You will try, but when things get tough, which they will, and you feel the pressure, you will plummet to your backup plan and never look at your dream ever again.

However, trust isn't something you get overnight, or in a month. It comes slowly and can even be hard to see at first but when you put your 100%, you will be the best one day, the trick is in knowing that you need to show up every day.

The road that you walk on is important because taking risks is important, but you need to know your risk-to-reward ratio. Only take risks if you think the reward in the end is worth taking a chance for. You need to know that when you commit to something, you will consign your freedom and time to that particular skill set. If you don't think, the person you will turn out after this long and tedious journey is someone you look up to now and whose life you really want to have. Then, it is simply not worth it.

You get a thousand shots at being above average, but only one shot at mastery. So you need to choose wisely.

Here is a table to Rank your current skills from best to worst. You are only allowed to choose four skills.

Skill Name	How Good are You At it?

Choose between Very Good, Good, Better than Average, Average

If you find skills that you chose "Good" or "Very Good" at, you have hit the jackpot. Those are the skills you need to double down on no matter if people try to talk you out of it, saying there isn't any scope in that field.

Remember, there are no good jobs but rather how good are you at your job. You need to learn to be the star in your field rather than chase the trendy jobs.

If you have skills that you are only average or better than average at, there is still hope for you. 6 months is all it really takes to cross each level. So technically, if you are average at something, after 6 months of dedicated practice, you will level up to being better than average. Why this works, is because 90% of people quit in the first 3 - 4 Months. So once you survive the 6-month mark, you will level up, provided you do the work with discipline rather than counting the days.

If you are better than average, the time is multiplied by 3. So technically, after your initial six months. You need another 18 months of practice to be good at something. This time will obviously vary, depending on your efforts, but on average, you will be able to see these time frames work for you.

EXPERIENCE EVERYTHING

Experience Failure, Experience Struggle, Experience Feeling Passion, Experience Getting Bored. Mastery is a journey that can leave you both in euphoria as well as frustration. You need to be mentally prepared for good days, bad days, and everything in between. In this chapter, we will cover just that so that you know what to expect.

The key to mastery is repetition and dedication. Let me already tell you that it isn't as easy as it sounds. That is why I am here to break it down for you.

The thing you need to understand is that there is no secret sauce except obsession. If I wasn't obsessed enough to finish this book, you wouldn't be reading it. I can say that practice every day and wrap this chapter up, but there is a lot more to it. Practice every day might have worked in the past when we didn't have many distractions like phones, laptops, or those weird Apple headsets. But in this era, where our attention span is less than a goldfish. Mastery is a harder challenge because it takes true willpower to tell yourself, "Listen you need to work on this thing and get better at it". In this world of instant gratification, practising delayed gratification is harder than ever. Since we can never know for sure what the future will look like if we work hard today, we just don't feel like it. Let me be honest here: I don't even know if a single soul will read my book. I just write it out of the fear of failure. I fear that if I don't finish this book, I will never know if it will work out in the end. Completion of the task is more important than whether the task is successful or not. I am 21 and honestly not doing the best financially, so I fear that writing this book is the last shot I have at living a decent life.

The road to mastery is a fearful one. Most of you reading this book weren't born with a silver spoon in your mouth. Still, you dared to dream and rebel against the life you were given. So I want you to fear losing it all.

Every time you feel like quitting, I want you to imagine how empty life would be without this skill that you are trying so hard to learn. I want you to think of it as your last hope for redemption. I know thinking about how successful you will be is a rosy answer, but rosy doesn't make us want to work hard. Only when we are scared shitless about where we might end up if we don't work hard today shall we realise the true value of our goals. Our mindset can never be "It would be nice if I achieved that". Rather, it has to be, "If I don't achieve that, I am doomed, and it is the end of the road for me". Mastery is something you should need rather than crave. Only then will you ever be able to walk the tough path.

It won't be fun. You will explore failures, just like everybody else who has tried to become something the world told them they were never meant to be. Remoulding yourself takes pressure. The down days today are the days left between you and your success.

A mix of fear and obsession that is almost psychotic is the trick to mastery. I said it, and I stand by it. Most of us aren't naturally talented at anything, so our unfair advantage needs to be our drive to do things. When you take all your disadvantages and turn them into your drive to do something, nobody can stop you.

Another thing you will experience in your road to mastery is finding flaws in yourself. You will take a good look at yourself and doubt your abilities, no matter how good you are. That is because we seek external validation to see our progress, and we all have a voice in our head saying, "Maybe you aren't as good as you imagined". We can't ignore this voice, so we are better off acknowledging it. Tackling the problem then and there is better than suppressing the problem and letting it build up. Life is just taking problems and finding better solutions to those problems.

Another feeling you will experience when you try to break your shell and try to master something is detachment. You will begin to detach from friends, family, your job, and maybe every other thing that is important to you. You will begin to create your own world with the creations that you are proud of. You will learn to compose your thoughts and spend a lot of time with them. The journey to the top is always a lonely one. Most people don't dare to dream of mastery as it takes so much time, dedication, and sacrifice. Dreaming big takes guts and a lot of self-belief. When you expect nothing less than actually achieving your dream, then you need to come to terms with the reality of the effort it is going to take.

Mastery of something will also most definitely lead to comparison. The great Irfaan Khan had said in an interview once that he always wondered why his hard work wasn't paying off even though his fellow actors were growing much faster than him. Even Greats doubt the process and question everything. Then how can you expect yourself to be sane? Mastery requires a little bit of insanity, as it isn't meant for everyone.

KNOW WHY

While pursuing mastery, two ideas need to tarry in your mind. The idea of consumption and the idea of creation. A common piece of advice you must have heard is to copy everything while trying to learn. I am here to tell you that this advice is absolutely right. We have come to a point in life where no idea is really original anymore. They are always inspired by others and improve. So, while you try to master a skill, all you really need to focus on is copying and improving. Once you are able to do that, you will understand that great ideas are just old ideas in different forms and mediums. Even this book, for example, do you really think nobody has written a book on learning new skills? Of course, they have, but I found them lacking the record of a journey. I am no know-it-all, but I only preach based on what I have observed through my life experiences. This obviously can never be the same for every person, which makes my idea original even if I am telling you what others have already said through my own lens.

What should I copy?

Should I copy everything in my field? Or should I copy only a few things? How do I find the right things to copy? Let me answer all these questions you may have. Well, the truth is you don't need to copy a trendy idea or something that you don't really have much to add to; otherwise, what is the point of your effort if you can't really add much to it? So, a better approach would be to consume things in which you are genuinely interested. Then, copy a few ideas from all over the place. Trust me, the key to an original idea is the randomness by which it is inspired. You should be warned, though, that only copy the ideas you resonate with; this will help you build upon them. Soon, when you try messing around with these ideas, you will start the experimentation phase. Here, you will realise that these ideas are somewhat incomplete, and I can expand on them. Not all of your experiments will be accepted by society. Here is where you need to be bold; the process of mastery is only to create new ideas; if you fail to do that because of fear of not being accepted, then you have officially wasted many years of your life.

If you are still reading, you have probably crossed the point of above average. From now on, all that matters is how authentic you are to yourself and in your skill set.

How Sensory Deprivation Works

The best trick to consume quality knowledge while simultaneously forming new ideas is "Boredom". What, how would that help? For me to prove my theory. I want you to think about a closed room. You are in that room. No phones, no tabs, no people to talk to. Just a notebook and a pen. All you can hear is silence. You sit there for 5 minutes. You sit there for 10 minutes, and 15 minutes have passed. The notebook is blank because you are just too lazy to write anything. After 20 minutes, you can't take it anymore. You pick up the pen and write the words "I am Bored". Now, I want you to take a step back and think about the skill you are trying to master. You flip the page and write the heading "How do I get better at (your skill)?" Thirty minutes pass by, and you write 5 points on how you could get better at something you have been trying so hard for. Now, writing that also becomes exhausting, so you toss your notebook and start screaming, "Open the Door, Let me out". No response. You cry and yell. Another 30 minutes pass and your brain is numb. You need something to keep you going. The absence of any stimulation is driving you crazy. Then suddenly, you are let out of that room and move to another room just like the one you came from, except this one has everything you need to practice your skills. It's almost like a eureka moment for you. You feel the ideas just rushing in your brain. You are in the zone, and time passes by so quickly that by the time you are exhausted from working on your new great ideas, it is noon. This room opens, and you are free to go. You are refreshed and relaxed. The next day, when you review your idea, 9 times out of 10, you will find out that the idea was pretty good. Since you now have the base, all you really need to do is build on it.

What I just described to you was the stimulation response. When you are completely deprived of stimulation, your brain tries to stimulate you through your thoughts after an hour of being deprived and just constantly thinking of your skill. You allow your brain to process past learnings and create new ideas. After being deprived of most pleasure responses like your phone, if you work on the skill you are good at, it becomes your pleasure response, and you immediately feel more motivated and in the zone. It's a hard thing to practice but very efficient and rewarding in the long run. You don't need to do this every week, but even once a week can produce great results.

Another thing that you can do, which is quite simple but effective, is creative breakdowns. This is only possible at a fairly advanced stage, but you can try deconstructing the most popular works. You can do this in your head or try doing it from scratch. How do I do this in my head? Take a piece of art, code, or music. Try finding out the techniques the creator has used and do a mental breakdown. If you can't figure it out then and there, study the technique and learn it. This small deconstruction strategy can help you learn as well as know your level of mastery in a certain skill.

CLEAR TIME

Time is something we always feel like we don't have enough of, and from this chapter, hell starts. I will tell you why. At this point, you are tired and just have no hope of moving forward. You will start to find yourself in situations where you think that you just can't give enough time to your skill. It sucks, doesn't it? You know you can be better at something but just aren't able to give 100% because of your environment. Maybe you have homework, or a job, or a family to take care of. You just don't see how you could ever get any better. Well, this is the time when you feel stranded, and success just looks like a mirage. Will you ever get there despite your efforts? Well, if you give up now, you will never know.

You pushed for years, didn't you? Made sacrifices and felt like you missed out on everything. Was all of that worth giving up now? No!. So you need to trust yourself and clear time. I know it's not easy to go the extra mile when your feet are bleeding, but if it was easy to master something, then wouldn't everyone do that? Clear time from your schedule. Two or three hours, that's all. If you are wondering how you will get that time, the truth is that you need to sacrifice your breaks; you need to treat the skill you are trying to master like a break. Only then could you ever master it. There will come a time when you get so good at something that doing it makes you feel happy. Unfortunately, getting to that stage requires hardships. Well, we all have limited time on this planet. It's up to us to be like everyone else or redefine ourselves.

Hope is something that will help you through this journey. Don't try to envision where you will be, but rather, try to envision where you were before. That will give you the real perspective of things that you so badly need at this stage. People will most definitely call you crazy when you tell them that you spend 3 or 4 hours on your skill. They will tell you it's an unhealthy obsession. Well, they never knew what it feels like to be so dedicated to something that you are ready to leave every little distraction this world has to offer. Mastery doesn't just teach you the skill, but it also teaches you life skills like patience, discipline, and making an effort to get where you want to be. Working on it is the only solution I can offer you because the mind needs a chance to unlock its full potential. This will take a lot of time, and it's going to feel like hell.

Sometimes, I think to myself, one day, I will be dead, and it won't matter if I was a master at something. Then another thought sets me free, saying that even if you die, your work will make you immortal. It's true; in this era, mastering something is very, very hard. So many talented people are overlooked, and even getting to that point seems so far when we have distractions every waking moment. What do we do? We can't throw our phones away. We can't just quit our jobs and practice one thing for the rest of our lives. We can't cut off the world and obsess over our skills. So don't try to do what you can't. Maybe there are no shortcuts to mastery. No tricks of the trade except struggling with people who are also in your position. It's sad that most of us won't ever be exceptionally good at one thing. Most will never taste fame, be rich, or travel the world. We won't have mansions, but all we will have is the feeling that tells us that, well, at least I am good at this.

Maybe all our lives are just based on chance. We may succeed, or we may never be heard. People may read my book or never glance at it. It's not in my control, so even after you try doing everything right, there is no guarantee that you will win. Does that mean I should be okay with working so hard when I have nothing waiting for me on the other side? Well, the truth is that once you start working on something you really are passionate about, you can't stop even if you see no results. We all are just people trying to write our own stories, and time will either help us get there or help us accept that maybe it's okay to be relatively unknown. I recently heard a quote that went like this, "Success doesn't care about your journey. It only cares how good you are at something". That's the truth. We can work the hardest and still never have things our way or be as successful as some people.

With this book, I tried to find a method to this madness: why are seemingly normal people so good at something while we struggle to even achieve 10% of that? I like to console myself by thinking that maybe in some universe, I am better than others. People say to work hard but don't realise that everyone has different definitions of hard. People have different responsibilities, problems, and lives. While I have failed to answer that question of how to master something, I have definitely done evident justice to the question "How to become above average at anything."

INVEST IN YOURSELF

As you get better at a skill, you will need to buy things to help you grow in it. A good photographer needs to invest in a good camera, and a musician in music equipment, and a good artist needs to invest in canvases and art equipment. There are two things that can happen when you do this. Either you will begin to feel guilty about your purchases or will face a small learning curve. In this chapter, let's try to get rid of the guilt associated with buying things to improve our skills.

I want you to understand that money is just a number. If you don't spend this money on improving yourself, then you will end up spending it on other unnecessary stuff. So why not buy things that you are passionate about? Most people in your life won't approve of your purchases and will call them useless. Just because others don't find it valuable, that doesn't mean it isn't valuable. When I bought my first camera, everyone told me that I was stupid to purchase it as all phones have cameras on them. Fast forward 3 years, that camera has led me to so many unexpected opportunities in life. I saw the potential of a camera when nobody else could, and that is what's important. Does this mean that I have never made an unnecessary purchase in my field of work? Of course, I have. I don't use some of the equipment I thought I would require, but the only way to know if your purchase was unnecessary is to try it out. Following a talent doesn't come cheap. You need to give it time as well as resources to get where you want to see yourself.

One trick I use is to only buy one item every 6 months, to improve my skills. In my filmmaking journey, I have wanted many things like fancy stands, lights, and lenses. This doesn't mean that I buy them all at once. This will just cause what I call a learning curve overload. Setting up all this new equipment will take up so much of your time in the initial stages that practising the actual skill becomes a nightmare.

Warren Buffet says, "Investing in yourself is the most important thing you can do". The best way to know which investments will actually be fruitful is to try asking people who are one level up or already using the equipment you are thinking of buying. People can be very helpful, especially if you share a common interest with them. All you need to do is be brave enough to ask so that you don't end up wasting money on shit you don't need. They might even agree to teach you how to use your new equipment if they are friendly. We can all always learn from each other. Today, I was at the gym, and even though I had been going there for two years straight, today, a stranger told me that my technique was wrong. I was annoyed at first, but when he showed it to me, I tried it. I realised that I was indeed wrong, and he was genuinely trying to help because he had made the same mistake a few years ago.

What If I Don't Have Money?

Pardon me for talking with my privileged lenses, but the truth is in India, we have talent but no one to fund our talents. It makes no sense that our parents are ready to pay for the top universities in the world but never pay attention to our hobbies and talents. Money is surely a barrier to entry in learning something new. But there is also a flip side to this. Since India is a developing economy, many things, like equipment and classes, cost less. You may have to use the good old savings method to get there, but what other choice do you have? Look at the bright side: when you don't have enough money to buy stuff to pursue your talents, it leads you to think outside the box and fight for your dream. You will never spend a dime on unnecessary equipment. The reality is that we never chase a dream until someone tells us not to. Restriction and constraint help set us free. Finding the way by yourself can be hard, but you will get there. Investing in yourself doesn't always mean money though, it also requires an investment of time. If you can't buy something with money, buy it with your time. Watch free tutorials and gain knowledge. You need to remember that the skill is more important than the equipment.

Recently, I was mentoring an underprivileged student, and we were figuring out skills he could build. Looking at his drive and creativity. We decided to explore graphic design, and then I told him to pivot to UI/ UX design. Even though he had no clue how to do it, he started out trusting the process. Just within 2 months of working on it, he has learned so much about Figma and UI/ UX processes. He didn't have to spend a dime to get that knowledge. If he had seen it as a setback and said I can't do this because I don't have the right equipment, then he would have never got this far. He gave the skill time rather than his money, and it is slowly paying off for him.

In the next chapter, I will teach you how to monetise your skills, as now you have stepped above what you thought you could achieve. Since you are spending money on perfecting your skills, it is only logical if you earn money with your newfound abilities. Don't you agree?. But remember, when you monetise your passion, you start to enjoy it less. So, only do this step if you feel like you also want a monetary benefit from what you learned.

MONEY! MONEY! MONEY!

Are you ready to make some money? You spent countless hours perfecting your craft, putting in time, resources, and effort. Now let's help you get off the ground and start making a living with your skill. Also congratulations on going above and beyond average. If you are still stuck there then give yourself some time.

Post Post Post

You don't live in the 19th century anymore, so take advantage of that. Finally, you are at a point where you can do cool stuff. The rule to creation is to always reveal your creations to the world. Some platforms that will help you are Instagram, LinkedIn, and Behance. You can either talk about your skills or let your work do the talking. Honestly, anything is fine as long as you project it to the world. What is the point of this, you may ask? Well, when you put your work out there, opportunities start coming to you. It will definitely take time. Even if you are skilled, it takes time for people to truly understand your work and appreciate it. You will be surprised how far posting once or twice a week in niche-specific groups can get you. While we are on the topic of social media. Another thing you need to do along with posting is outreach.

> **Steal this template:**
>
> Hi (enter name of person), I really liked your work in (a very specific project they worked on) I actually had a question (Ask them a very specific question about something you are curious about), I understand that you are busy and it's ok if you don't respond. Thank you for your time.
>
> If it's an email then use the subject: (Your Name) (Phone number)

This template will help you unlock so many doors. You need to be consistent and always keep at it.

When someone wants to work with you

When someone approaches you and is on board with the idea of working with you, you need to focus on the value you provide rather than your price. If the client starts to negotiate on price, let them know that your prices are justified because you will provide them with so and so skills. These skills are unique to you and cannot be replicated. Sometimes, you may find the wrong people as well, who will exploit you and pay you less. It is always better to say no to such opportunities in search of better ones.

While applying your skills for money, you need to learn a few things including negotiation and a system. Most working professionals have a built-in system that helps them give out maximum output in minimum time. Usually, this comes with experience but a rough plan in your head definitely helps out. Remember that the money may not start rolling in immediately but this shouldn't be a cause of stress and anxiety. You need to be confident in yourself to know how to grow.

As long as you are putting yourself out there through your socials and reaching out to people. You will eventually start landing gigs, 'cause remember. You are not average anymore, you are better than most people, making what you have to offer also special.

Trust

Oftentimes, it is the greats that are filled with self-doubt. We never think that we are good enough. It is probably because to get to that point took a long time and a lot of criticism. Everyone is insecure, and that's ok. There was an experiment conducted where five average-looking people were called into the room, and five good-looking people were also present in the room. They each were given a sheet of paper and a pen. The person conducting the experiment came into the room and told both groups of people to write about their flaws. The results were shocking; the good-looking people listed down more flaws than the average-looking people. How is this relevant to us? When you become good at something you begin to notice even the smallest of mistakes invisible to the untrained eye. This endless strive for perfection can ultimately lead to your downfall. So, once you are good at something, try to find the joy of exploring it rather than being a perfectionist. It is the time to experiment and discover, not find flaws and crumble.

Know your Worth

You aren't worthless, I repeat, **"YOU AREN'T WORTHLESS"**. So don't go around letting people decide how much your time is worth. You need to let them know instead. There are only two kinds of people. People who genuinely value your work and people who just want to exploit you. It might seem obvious to go with the first kind, but most people fall into the desperation trap. They just can't bring themselves to say **NO** to the second group of people. Think of it this way: every time you reluctantly work for someone, you miss out on working with someone who appreciates you. Just like how you don't go out with the first person who asks you out, you have to learn to take on the right clients and choose the right opportunities. How do you find the right opportunities? The first step is to understand why someone wants to work with you. Is it because of your quality of work and the value you provide or because they were looking for someone to hire that may or may not be you? Always give more importance to the first opportunity, even if the pay may be slightly lower. Sometimes, we run after the money but end up with horrible working conditions or, worse, micro-managers. If you have trained for years to learn a skill, you can't expect someone to micromanage you and interfere with every creative decision you make. It is just wasteful and frustrating.

YOU DID IT

If you are reading this chapter. "HOLY FUCKING SHIT". I just wrote an interesting book to keep you reading till the end. But there is one thing I have been saving for you that will be a great end to this book. First of all, if you did the things I said and are reading the book as you progress each level of your journey. Then congratulations, you made it. You started with absolutely no idea how to take something; you didn't even think you were good at, and you turned yourself into someone who can now proudly say that you are better than most people at it. Now, most of you may not make it to mastery; neither did I. Because that takes decades of dedication, and either we take a lot of time to get there or just don't feel like progressing that far into the journey. That is completely ok. The point of the book was to take any skill and make you better than most people at it. Going from "Better" to "Best" is just following the cycle again and again till you get there.

Here is a table for you to write where you were with your skill at the beginning of the book and where you are now (Assuming you followed everything I said and gave it time to show its magic). If you are one of those people who reads a book within a day. Then maybe leave this space blank for now and reread the book in 6 months and fill the table. It's a self-help book, so I can just show you the path, but you have to walk the walk all by yourself.

GIVE YOURSELF TIME BEFORE YOU FILL THIS SECTION

Skill	Where I Was Before Using the Advice in this Book	Where I am Now

Here Is My List
(in the last 2 years)

Skill	Where I Was Before Using the Advice in this Book	Where I am Now
Chess	Was at 700 Rating	Reached my 1k goal and stopped for a while
Guitar	Started with playing simple guitar tabs	Now I can play amateur-level tabs and songs on the guitar
Singing	Had an intolerable Voice	Have reached a stage where people tolerate my singing. Still not at a "wow level" but working on it
Drawing	Had a goal to draw portraits.	Haven't been working on that goal and haven't dedicated the time required

Video Editing	Knew basic editing and wanted to learn colour grading	Learned colour grading and cinematography and now make around 25k with video editing

As you can see from my list, these are not miracle results in any way. There was one goal I didn't give time to, a few where work is still required, and one that I achieved. So don't get disappointed when your results aren't out of this world. Know that knowledge is only useful when you put it into practice. In 80% of the table, you can see progress being made. That is how learning is. You can't expect this table to be 100% if you do everything honestly. Sometimes, we just don't see ourselves as excited about diving further into a topic like before, and that is ok. It is okay to leave some goals behind if you feel like you don't want them in your current lifestyle.

A life of growth is a hard one indeed. After all, we would love to sit on the couch and envy those who "made it" rather than take the first step toward our growth. I believe that deep down, we all know the exact recipe for success, but they are suppressed by things like self-doubt, laziness, or even the constant victimisation of yourself. I have a friend who I personally think is very talented, but I never wish to be like him as he sees the world in such a negative light and always talks about change but never changes. I never used to understand those kinds of people, but then it dawned upon me that everyone is aware of what they should be doing but never actually do it.

Over the years, I have pushed myself and realised that the more you do, the more momentum you create, and the subconscious urge to maintain your progress is born. The opposite is also true: the less you do, the less motivation you feel, and you succumb to your mind telling you that it's not worth it since you are so far behind. Have I ever faced that voice telling me this exact thing? Fuck yes, and the only way to deal with this is to start and see where it gets you. There was no magic mantra there; being behind was never the challenge, not taking the first step was. That's the main reason I named this book "The Average Man" because I never intended for you to feel like you were behind or could never make it in life. My intention was to show you that even though I started by being below average, taking that first step really helped me get to where I am today. I have tried to share what I have learned with you with as much transparency as possible. The last chapter is very important so I suggest you read it.

WORLD CLASS

For the last 2 years of my life, I have dreamed of one day writing the last chapter of this book. I never thought this day would come, and honestly, it wouldn't have if I hadn't had an enlightening conversation with my girlfriend's elder sister. I wanted the ending of this book to be perfect in every way and waited for perfection to come to me. I first waited for a week, then 2 weeks, and soon those 2 weeks turned into 4, and here I am a month later. I am here to tell you that the wait was irrational. The reason

I just couldn't get myself to write the last chapter was because ends are hard. It's much easier to start something than to go all the way and finish it. It would have never mattered what I wrote because I had convinced myself that it wouldn't be good enough to be the end. Then I realised that oftentimes, we are so hard on ourselves that we forget why we started in the first place.

So what was it that my girlfriend's sister told me that got me so fired up to finish this chapter that very night? She told me that perfection was an illusion. This might seem like an obvious statement to someone just getting started, but for someone who has crossed all the hurdles to be good enough at something, it never feels complete. When you have learned almost everything there is to learn, you will question everything you learned and lust for more to do. You will forget that mastery can only do so much. It is up to you to fearlessly create when you reach that level. All the famous personalities out there probably had their own stories, where somebody put a hand on their shoulder and said, "Just do it, because if you don't, then you will regret it forever."

Perfection is a mindset; if you enjoy what you create, then it's perfect. If you don't practice gratitude on this journey of learning, then you will always feel inadequate. The human mind can show you things through the lenses you choose. If you see yourself confidently, you are confident. If you see yourself as someone who doubts each and every step, you are diffident and need encouragement. Just because you are now good at a skill doesn't mean you can be world-class. You can only be world-class if you change your lenses and see yourself as worthy of being world-class. That's the only secret. It isn't hard work or determination that separates the good from the great; it is the belief in their ability that draws the line. The more you believe, the more you achieve.

I believe that someday I will sing my song to the world, and I believe that someday this book will be a worldwide bestseller. Even though I am an atheist, I think the power of manifestation is really true. Just letting the universe know that you want something is enough to help you get there. Show yourself a glimpse of who you can be inside your head. Humans are gifted with a superpower called imagination that can help you see things that aren't there yet. So use it.

Everyone has a dream, but very few have an aim. So, my intention with the book is to turn you from a dreamer into an aimer. An aim is achieved by breaking down your steps into small, digestible tasks. You can only become world-class by the repetition of these small digestible tasks so that with each day, you get better at it than you were.

You never know if you will make it in this world filled with competition, but you can surely try. It took

Ed Sheeran 4 years to go from sounding like a screeching goat to one of the most melodic voices ever. Talent is in there. You need to get it out and let it shine.

I hope this book helped you learn the tips and tricks of learning and made a difference in your life. It's 2:10 am on a Saturday right now, and even though I have no idea how to end a book or write a perfect chapter, I think I have finally done it. I finally finished writing my book, and you finally finished reading it. So, if this book ever does change your life, I would love for you to write to me. Remember that we all are average until we take the first step.

The End

Acknowledgement

Firstly, I would like to thank my hunger for getting out of this average life. Now, let's actually acknowledge the beautiful people who kept me going. A big thank you to my girlfriend and graphic designer, Bhumi Agrawal, for creating such an impactful book cover for *The Average Man*. Next, I would like to thank Pavithra. S. Kumar, Swayam Kumar and Chandramauli Singh, for their valuable feedback during the initial stages of the book. The reason I published this book was because my brother helped me fight the self-doubt that came with publishing, so a big thank you to Sarthak Tripathy for always being there for me. I would also like to thank Devaraju Kousik Sai from Notion Press for his helpful guidance and insight in helping this book get published. I would like to extend my gratitude to Sunayan Sarkar for helping me market this book and get it out to all my readers. Lastly, I would like to thank you, yes "You", for reading this book. I would like to thank you for taking the courage to change your life for the better. Not many people are brave enough to beat the average life and push themselves to be a better person. I hope this book gives you the answers you are looking for and helps you understand your true potential.

www.ingramcontent.com/pod-product-compliance
Lightning Source LLC
Chambersburg PA
CBHW030054110726
47973CB00002B/13